# FEAR IN THE AIR

*Broadcasting and the First Amendment:*
*The Anatomy of a Constitutional Crisis*

# FEAR IN THE AIR

Broadcasting and the First Amendment:
The Anatomy of a Constitutional Crisis

by Harry S. Ashmore

W·W·NORTON & COMPANY·INC·New York

Copyright © 1973 by W. W. Norton & Company, Inc.
FIRST EDITION

Library of Congress Cataloging in Publication Data
Ashmore, Harry S.
   Fear in the air.
1. Liberty of the press—United States.
2. Television—Law and legislation—United States.
3. Radio—United States—Laws and regulations.
I. Title.
KF4774.A98        342′.73′085        73–12213
ISBN 0–393–08368–3

Printed in the United States of America

1 2 3 4 5 6 7 8 9 0

*For*

## WILLIAM BENTON

*whose Benton Foundation made possible the conference at the Center for the Study of Democratic Institutions upon which this volume is based. Bill Benton devoted a share of his prodigious energy and personal resources to the ideal of the First Amendment until the day of his death, March 18, 1973. The necessity of maintaining the health of the free press by opening its own performance to what the courts call robust criticism occupied him through his several careers as advertising agency principal in the pioneering days of broadcasting, as university vice-president, as Assistant Secretary of State for Information, as United States senator, and as publisher of the* Encyclopaedia Britannica. *When Henry R. Luce's patience and financing ran out for the old Commission on the Freedom of the Press, Bill Benton put up his own funds to publish its findings. He helped finance the Twentieth Century Fund committee that revived the idea a quarter of a century later in the form of the National News Council. I am one of many journalists he left in his debt.*

# CONTENTS

# FEAR IN THE AIR

Broadcasting and the First Amendment:
The Anatomy of a Constitutional Crisis

# CHAPTER 1

# NEW CHALLENGE
# TO AN OLD IDEAL

*The key to the . . . feud between the Nixon administration and the news media may lie in legal and economic history. Quite simply: Is the First Amendment to the United States Constitution obsolescent . . . ? My own feeling is yes, the Amendment is obsolescent and therefore cannot cope with Big Media power. This invites—and even obliges—the government to move in. . . .*
—Kevin P. Phillips

BEFORE THE Watergate scandals gave the Nixon administration its comeuppance, leaders of the communications industry had come to accept this statement as an accurate reflection of the attitude of the President and his inner circle of White House advisers, among whom Kevin Phillips has served as a political tactician. Subsequent changes in the palace guard have provided no reason to believe that the Phillips dictum has been superseded— although the President's ability to implement it may have been somewhat reduced since the days when his surrogates rallied a broad public response with their onslaught against an effete eastern seaboard liberal intellectual establishment they claimed had seized control of the media.

The attack, actually intensified after the President's overwhelming reelection, no doubt took some coloration from Mr. Nixon's personal ambitions and peculiar trauma. But the give-and-take around the Watergate issue also served to bring into relief the profoundly altered pattern of relationships between the government and what used to be called the press. These changes are the product, not of presidential pique, but of the imperatives of a new electronic age.

While the newspapers, and most notably the *Washington Post*, led the counterattack, the main thrust of the White House effort was aimed at the broadcasters. Initially, the print media tended to shrug off with amused tolerance the rhetorical broadsides from the campaign forces led by Vice-President Spiro Agnew. But executives of the commercial TV networks complained that they were being subjected not merely to public chastisement but to direct and indirect pressures to bring their news and public affairs programming into line with the Nixon administration's highly selective view of what the public should see and hear. Walter Cronkite of CBS identified an "orchestrated, coordinated campaign . . . agreed upon in secret by members of the administration" and traced it as far back as 1969, when Vice-President Agnew in a speech in Des Moines first labeled the TV commentators "a tiny, enclosed fraternity of privileged men elected by no one and enjoying a monopoly sanctioned and licensed by government." Dependent as they are upon the radio and TV stations they own or franchise, the networks could only regard this as a pointed reminder that each of these outlets remains on the air only under official sufferance.

Over a period of many months seismic tremors were systematically engendered along Madison Avenue by official and semi-official pronouncements carrying with them unmistakable threats to the phenomenal income and profit curve of the three networks—which in 1972 showed a gross of $1.6 billion, profits of $213.4 million before taxes, and a resounding 47.2 percent earnings gain over 1971. By early January 1973 a round-up in the financial section of the *Los Angeles Times* reported "a massive case of government-induced tension and chills" among network executives: "They view the Administration's antinetwork campaign—emanating piecemeal from the Federal Communications Commission, the Federal Trade Commission, the Justice Department, and the White House itself—partly as retribution for broadcasters' failure to toe the Nixon line in their news and feature programming."

Aside from the frontal assault on the integrity of network news operations, there were three moves aimed directly at the pocketbook nerve—a civil antitrust suit by the Justice Department intended to force the networks out of the programming business; a proposal by FTC to require broadcasters to sell, and in some cases to give away, "counteradvertising" to persons and organizations wishing to attack specific commercials; and a move by FCC to drastically curtail the number of program reruns. Any one of these proposals could spell financial disaster for the networks, and they were timed to coincide with a move from the White House itself to weaken the networks' position in relation to their affiliated stations. Chairman Robert Sarnoff of NBC saw in this a pattern aimed at impeding the flow of information from the nation's major news medium by "increasing a network's costs, disrupting its operations, and reducing its economic opportunities."

The pincers movement against the networks began to attract general public attention in early 1972, when Patrick Buchanan of the White House staff publicly suggested that an antitrust approach to network news programming might have to be developed to counter what he described as "an ideological monopoly." This thesis appeared to receive a formal imprimatur when Clay T. Whitehead, director of the White House Office of Telecommunications Policy, set forth the outlines of proposed administration legislation designed to affect the relationship between the unlicensed networks and their licensed local outlets.

In a speech before the professional journalism fraternity, Sigma Delta Chi, Whitehead charged that broadcasters were remiss in maintaining adequate standards of taste, violence, and decency, and in guaranteeing "reasonable, realistic, and practical opportunities for the presentation and discussion of conflicting views on controversial issues." He located the principal reason for this dereliction in the failure of the local stations to exercise responsibility for the 61 percent of programming the average affiliate accepts as it "comes down the network pipe."

"The station owners and managers cannot abdicate responsibility for news judgment," Whitehead said. "When a reporter or disc jockey slips in or passes over information in order to line his pocket that's plugola, and management would take quick corrective action. But men also stress or suppress information in accordance with their beliefs. Will station licensees or network executives also take action against this ideological plugola?" Whitehead answered his own question by asserting that the inability of network executives to guarantee against ideological pollution is so manifest that the local licensees, under the prod of the FCC, must assume the obligation. He dismissed the possibility of constitutional conflict:

"The First Amendment's guarantee of a free press was not supposed to create a privileged class of men called journalists who are immune to criticism by government or restraint by publishers and editors. To the contrary, the working journalist, if he follows a professional code of ethics, gives up the right to present his personal point of view when he is on the job. . . . He realizes he has no monopoly on the truth; that a pet view of reality can't be insinuated into the news. . . . Who else but management can or should correct so-called professionals who confuse sensationalism with sense and who disperse elitist gossip in the guise of news analysis?"

Kevin Phillips cites the Whitehead statement as an example of the Nixon administration's conviction that the public interest requires that this "adversary culture" be curbed:

"Never before has any country's intelligentsia, or 'knowledge industry,' been big enough and rich enough to create an important separate culture hostile to the nation's prevalent middle-class values—and the New York–Washington media axis is the linchpin of this unique elite. . . . It is fair to say that the Administration's target is not the press *per se* but a special subculture without socio-economic precedent in the annals of American power."

The righteous fervor that lies behind this indictment is indicated in Phillips' contemptuous dismissal of the argument that under American tradition and constitutional theory the government is free to criticize, but not to overtly interfere with the functioning of the free press:

"Not surprisingly, the subculture is trying to portray its fight as one for the 'people's right to know.' Phooey! What people's right to know what information? Joe Suburbanite's right to know how the Department of Health, Education, and Welfare's bureaucracy coddles busing, or how the Vietnam mess was originally blueprinted by foundation and Ivy League liberals, or how liberal profiteers are making fortunes off subsidized housing, poverty programs, and environmental consulting businesses? Hell, no. You never see that kind of investigation in the big liberal media. 'The people's right to know' is a code for the Manhattan Adversary Culture's desire to wrap the First Amendment around its attack on the politicians, government, and institutions of Middle America."

This populist coloration shows up in Whitehead's proposed cure for the derelictions of the networks. Legislation drafted in the White House would not only emphasize the station owner's total responsibility for everything he puts on the air, but prescribe that, wherever a program might originate, it must conform to *local* standards of taste and political outlook. Station owners would be rewarded for assuming the burden with a provision that licenses can be renewed for a term running for five years, instead of the present three, once the applicant has "demonstrated that he has been substantially attuned to the needs and interests of the communities he serves."

Whitehead contends that his proposed bill would not confer any powers on FCC it doesn't already have, nor establish any new responsibility for local licensees. Yet the tone of his statements, and the results claimed for proposed changes, have convinced the networks that the legislation is a punitive move designed to complicate their relationship with the member stations, and thereby reduce their independence and effectiveness in the area of news and public affairs.

No one familiar with the record can doubt that most station owners, given an open choice, would opt for the networks' brand of bland common denominator entertainment, which is highly profitable, rather than the news and documentaries generated by the networks' able national and international staffs. The best of public affairs programming, notably the distinguished documentaries, attracts little advertising revenue and must be written off as a "loss leader."

This not only returns no profit to the stations but is likely to stir up local controversy for which few station owners have any real stomach. To strengthen the stations' leverage on the network schedule, the *Washington Post* contends, "is to blunt the critical inquisitiveness of the network news organizations—with the threat of governmental reprisal at the end of the line. Under the pretext of eliminating bias, and in the guise of our First Amendment rights, the Administration is proposing to set the local affiliates or, failing that, itself up as the ultimate arbiter of the truth to which the public is to be exposed."

Paralleling the move against the commercial networks, the White House in the flush of its reelection victory acted directly to virtually emasculate the public affairs operations of the fledgling public television network that came into being only four years ago. In late 1972 Mr. Nixon vetoed the public system's annual appropriation, and revamped the controlling board to replace the president of the Corporation for Public Broadcasting with a loyal bureaucrat of his own choice. The reorganization prompted the protest resignations of key personnel and caused the retiring chairman of the Public Broadcasting Service to declare the non-commercial network effectively defunct as a source of critical reporting on national public affairs, and as a needed national forum for unconventional views.

The controversy between the Nixon administration and the national media flared against a backdrop of shifting legal interpretation of the First Amendment to the United States Constitution. The genesis is in these few words:

"Congress shall make no law respecting the establishment of religion, or prohibiting the free exercise thereof; or abridging the freedom of speech or of the press; or the right of the people peaceably to assemble, and to petition the Government for a redress of grievances."

To a layman the language seems immutable and clear; the government shall in no way inhibit the dissemination of ideas and argument. It follows that the rights conferred by the First Amendment lie in the realm of attitude, mode, and tone as well as in the guarantee of expression—that is, in the ability to feel secure in exercising the right to worship, speak, publish, assemble, and petition. Free thought no less than free speech is at stake, since a separation of the two leaves the first practically meaningless.

It is reasonable to assume that, in the context of their time, the men who fashioned the First Amendment would have considered any form of licensing of the press a clear violation of their intent. When the government, for the first time, moved in that direction with the allocation of radio broadcast channels, an elaborate legal formula was evolved to avoid violating the constitutional proscription against censorship. It has never been entirely satisfactory, and now it has come under attack from all sides.

The premise for governmental regulation of broadcasting, as distinguished from other media, is technological scarcity. Since a finite number of bands are available for voice and visual transmission, access to the spectrum must be limited if the public is to receive clear and discrete signals. These technological imperatives created the necessity for licensing, and with it a potential for direct governmental leverage on this sector of the privately owned communications system.

Rick J. Carlson, research attorney and Visiting Fellow at the Center for the Study of Democratic Institutions, has summarized the principles embodied in the law as it now applies to the communications media:

The First Amendment bars the Congress from promulgating any law which abridges freedom of speech. It is public action, not private action, which is prohibited, and the ban extends to all levels of government.

There are exceptions to this proscription. These include, to varying degrees, obscenity, defamation, and incitement to breach of peace. In these cases the Supreme Court has declined to adopt an "absolute" reading of the Amendment. Instead, the Court has fashioned tests to determine whether certain speech would be protected, i.e., the "clear and present danger" axiom against which certain "political" speech has been measured. A balancing theory has been used to determine whether the government's interest in suppressing speech was greater than the individual's right of expression.

While the First Amendment presumably applies to all forms of expression, the media are differently treated. No official body passes on the performance of the print media, while the Federal Communications Commission (FCC) has the function of balancing the interests of the broadcast media against the interests of the public. This is effectuated through a mandatory licensing scheme.

The FCC is required by law to ensure that licensees operate in the "public interest, convenience or necessity." However, the enabling act also specifically bars the FCC from exercising censorship. This apparent contradiction is the basis of the legal controversy that has arisen, and continues, over the extent and propriety of FCC interventions that affect program content.

The current focus is on the exercise of FCC supervisory power through the Fairness Doctrine, in effect since 1949. Broadcasters are required to afford a reasonable opportunity for the presentation of opposing views on controversial issues of public importance, or for reply in case of personal attack. The obligation rests with the broadcaster and is to be met by the licensee as he deems appropriate. The FCC interprets its mission as one of fixing guidelines and policing broadcaster implementation.

In 1968 the Supreme Court unanimously upheld the Fairness Doctrine against constitutional challenge in the *Red Lion* case.

The boundaries of that decision are currently in dispute among legal theorists. The Court directly sustained only the validity of the "personal attack" rules, which form a part of the Doctrine. However, the action served to vivify concepts not directly in question when the Court held that the right of viewers and listeners is paramount, not the right of the broadcaster.

Since *Red Lion*, two notable cases have passed through the U.S. Circuit Court of Appeals for the District of Columbia en route to the Supreme Court. On appeal from an FCC ruling, the Circuit Court upheld the challenge of Business Executives Move for Vietnam Peace (BEM) against network refusal to sell advertising time for the airing of a BEM documentary film setting forth its views on the Vietnam war. While conceding that the "right to speak" is subject to reasonable abridgment, the Court warned: "It is too late to argue that the First Amendment protects ideas, but not an individual's interest in expressing them and doing so in his own way."

In *Brandywine*, a unanimous Circuit Court opinion upheld the FCC's revocation of a Pennsylvania radio station's license under the Fairness Doctrine, finding the licensee guilty of "denial of an open and free air wave to the people of Philadelphia and its environs." The liberal Chief Judge, David Bazelon, later reversed himself and issued a dissenting opinion arguing that license revocation in itself may be a violation of the First Amendment, since the effect is to foreclose a voice from the air and deprive the public of the opportunity to hear *its* dissenting views. Since the only sanction the FCC applies in such cases is what amounts to capital punishment, Judge Bazelon thought he could detect a "chilling effect" on licensees, seeming "to move us a step backwards, away from the First Amendment marketplace ideal, in the name of the Fairness Doctrine."

The Supreme Court, in May 1973, reversed the appellate court in the *BEM* case and affirmed, seven to two, the broadcaster's right to refuse "editorial" advertising. For the majority, Chief Justice Warren E. Burger held that Congress had never intended that "broadcast facilities should be open on a nonselective basis to all persons wishing to talk about public issues." The two dissenting justices, William J. Brennan, Jr., and Thurgood Marshall, argued that the Fairness Doctrine, thus limited to political campaign matters and defamation, was insufficient "to provide the kind of uninhibited, robust, and wide-open exchange of views to which the public is constitutionally entitled."

Five separate concurring opinions demonstrated the wide range of reasoning on the obviously troublesome basic issue. One of these came from Justice William O. Douglas, on one of the rare occasions when he has departed the company of his liberal brethren to vote with the Chief Justice. Douglas followed the line suggested by Judge Bazelon in *Brandywine,* and went further than the Court has ever gone in upholding First Amendment rights for broadcasters:

"Television and radio stand in the same protected position under the First Amendment as do newspapers and magazines. . . . The Fairness Doctrine . . . puts the head of the camel inside the tent and enables administration after administration to toy with television or radio to serve its sordid or benevolent ends."

These cases demonstrate how far we have come since the First Amendment was simply cast as an absolute barrier to governmental censorship. It obviously has yielded to a degree now that the most pervasive and powerful communications medium can be compelled by government action to disseminate ideas and arguments promulgated by individuals and groups who under similar circumstances are assumed to have no such recourse in regard to the print media. In sum, the Fairness Doctrine can be said to have enhanced the ability of dissident groups to give voice to their views, but it also has raised the specter of the use of governmental authority as a means of eliminating or reducing the criticism of government postulated under the constitutional guarantee of freedom of the press.

Any attempt to forecast the future course of the law in these matters must take into account the current record of the final arbiter, the Supreme Court of the United States. In the years since Mr. Nixon took office, the Warren Court, so-called after Chief Justice Earl Warren, who led it to a high-water mark in the protection and expansion of civil liberties, has given way to a divided bench led by the President's first appointee, Warren Burger. The actuarial circumstance that the life terms of the justices tend to periodically produce a cluster in the upper age brackets (there have been only a hundred members of the Court since its inception) has already enabled Mr. Nixon to fill four out of the nine seats, and only the electronic pacemaker that steadies the heartbeat of the seventy-four-year-old Justice Douglas stands between the White House and a controlling majority.

Mr. Nixon has said that he intends to send to the bench only those who "share my conservative philosophy." How that has worked out in practice is attested by Louis M. Kohlmeier, Jr., in his new appraisal of the tribunal, *God Save This Honorable Court:* "Nixon politicized the Supreme Court more dramatically than any President in history." In the area of civil liberties and civil rights, the Burger Court has virtually brought to a halt the historic shift toward a full guarantee of social and economic as well as political equality for racial and ethnic minorities. "Skillfully, purposefully and politically," Kohlmeier writes, "Nixon converted the school bus from a symbol of equality into a symbol of racism."

In the first three years after the President laid his imprint on the Court with the appointment of the new Chief Justice, sixteen First Amendment cases were decided, involving claimed violations of the rights of speech, press, religion, and assembly. In 60 percent of these cases, the Court held that First Amendment protections had been violated, and ordered redress. The voting total was 78 yes, 52 no—but 61 of the pro-First Amendment votes were cast by four holdovers, against only 11 by the Nixon appointees. Justice White, who has become the Court's swing man, voted 6 for, 10 against.

Justices Douglas, Brennan, and Marshall upheld strict construction of the First Amendment with 100 percent of their votes, Stewart with 87 percent, and White with 38 percent. The Nixon appointees' score: Burger, 35 percent; Powell, 30 percent; Blackmun, 19 percent; and Rehnquist, 10 percent. Weighting those votes according to tendencies indicated in the Justices' formal opinions, Harold J. Spaeth of Michigan State University, who keeps tabs on the Supreme Court with a computer, reckons that the President's men on the bench are three times as likely to vote against a claim of First Amendment violation as they are for it.

When the Court recessed at the end of its 1972–73 regular term, the *Los Angeles Times* summarized the result of the "Nixonization" process: "His four appointees, in their first full term together on the Court, have remade the tribunal according to the specifications he gave them in appointing them to the bench. What has emerged is a Supreme Court . . . which rather consistently defers to the police, prosecutors, and state legislatures, comes down hard on criminals, and assumes a moralistic, straitlaced stance toward the

world." The somber implications of this record for the beleaguered mass media may be seen in the fact that the Nixon
appointees then on the Court not only made up a solid
minority in the celebrated *Pentagon Papers* case, but expressed themselves forthrightly as favoring the government's
claimed right of prior restraint on publication—the classic
exercise of official censorship every previous Court has declared abhorrent to the First Amendment.

# CHAPTER 2

# THE DIMENSIONS
# OF THE CONTROVERSY

AS THE SHAMBLES that was the 1972 presidential contest approached its foreordained conclusion, it seemed evident to Richard Salant, president of CBS News, that the Nixon administration's sustained attack on the mass media in general, and the commercial networks in particular, had gone past the point of no return and was not likely to subside once the votes were counted. Inquiring if the matter might be within the range of the continuing inquiry into the mass media that has sporadically occupied the Center for the Study of Democratic Institutions, Salant, a lawyer by training, stated the issue in these terms:

"The problem becomes increasingly urgent and increasingly difficult. The proper accommodation between the imperatives of a licensing system for broadcasting, on the one hand, and the First Amendment, on the other hand, is a subject which deserves and has not yet had the application and attention of the nation's best and most innovative minds. All it has received thus far, in general, is reflexive, automatic sloganeering by liberals and conservatives alike."

This was the genesis of a two-day conference on Broadcasting and the First Amendment at the Center in Santa Barbara at the end of January, 1973. With funding from the William Benton Foundation, the Center brought together a group of participants familiar in their own experience with the concerns of the commercial and public network news operations, the Nixon administration's approach to public affairs broadcasting, the regulatory practices of FCC, the view of leading First Amendment theorists, the record of practicing members of the Federal Communications Bar, and the disparate positions taken by the station owners. This covered the range of often conflicting interests involved in the increasingly uneasy relationship between government and the broadcasting industry. The public interest, with a spread of viewpoints equally wide, was represented by Fellows and Associates of the Center, many of whom are experienced in print and broadcast journalism as practiced in the United States and abroad. Also present, at the very beginning of his career as an independent arbiter in these matters, was the first chairman of the new, unofficial National News Council.

The conference quickly dashed Salant's hope that it might bring forth a "Bill of Rights" for broadcasting if it remained narrowly focused on the peculiar circumstances arising from the fact that one segment of the mass communications system is licensed and to some extent officially regulated, while the remainder presumably enjoys First Amendment protection against government intervention in its news and public affairs operations. In a prospectus for the conference prepared in early fall, I identified these central questions:

1. Does the fact that broadcasting is licensed, while the print media are not, abrogate the right of the people to receive public information and argument free of government intervention?
2. Have the special qualities of broadcast communication in-

troduced factors that justify a reconsideration of the standards previously accepted by the Supreme Court for the practice of journalism? Can the FCC's Fairness Doctrine, and more extended forms of right to access, be justified on this ground?

3. How is the presumed right of the FCC to require standards of performance by licensees limited by the First Amendment?

By the end of January events had overtaken this modest agenda. The collision between the White House and the media had spilled over into the courts, and had produced a set of side issues involving the relationship between the executive and legislative branches. New opinions had come down from the Supreme Court and the benches below. The President's men had taken control of the Corporation for Public Broadcasting and appeared bent on dismantling the noncommercial network. And the Twentieth Century Fund had announced that it would renew the effort to create an unofficial press council to deal with what appeared to be a mounting crisis reflected not only in the presidential vendetta but in the general public's declining confidence in the mass media. The First Amendment would remain at the core of the conference, but it was clear that the exploration would range far beyond the immediate question of its application to broadcasting.

Those who participated in the two-day discussion, and are quoted at some point throughout this book, were:

RICK J. CARLSON, Visiting Fellow and research attorney

BLAIR CLARK, former director of CBS News, Center board member

LLOYD CUTLER, Washington attorney, counsel to CBS

REUVEN FRANK, former president of NBC News

NORTON GINSBURG, dean of the Center, past president of the Association of American Geographers

ROBERT MAYNARD HUTCHINS, chairman of the Center, former dean of the Yale Law School, former president of the University of Chicago, chairman of the Commission on a Free and Responsible Press (1947)

HARRY KALVEN, JR., professor of law, University of Chicago

JAMES LOPER, president and general manager of KCET, Los Angeles, and former chairman of the Public Broadcasting Service

DONALD MCDONALD, executive editor of *The Center Magazine*

NEWTON MINOW, Chicago attorney, former FCC chairman

WENDELL MORDY, Visiting Fellow and professor of meteorology

FRED WARNER NEAL, Associate Fellow, professor of international relations, Claremont University Center and Graduate School

PAUL PORTER, Washington attorney, former FCC chairman

LORD RITCHIE-CALDER, Senior Fellow and Britain's leading science writer

LAWRENCE H. ROGERS II, president of the Taft Broadcasting Company

RICHARD SALANT, president of CBS News

ANTONIN SCALIA, former general counsel for the White House Office of Telecommunications Policy, now chairman of the Administrative Conference of the United States

RONALD M. SEGAL, Visiting Fellow, expatriate South African author and social critic

ERIC SEVAREID, CBS commentator

ROGER TRAYNOR, former Chief Justice of California, chairman of Twentieth Century Fund's National News Council

REXFORD GUY TUGWELL, Senior Fellow, former New Deal Brainstruster

HARVEY WHEELER, Senior Fellow, political scientist and author

HAROLD WILLENS, co-director of Business Executives Move
for Peace in Vietnam, director of the Center
THOMAS H. WOLF, vice-president in charge of TV documentaries, ABC News

The wide divergence of views between the Nixon administration and the networks, the ambivalence of many station
owners, and the confusion implicit in current interpretations
of the law were immediately established in the conference's
initial exchanges:

ANTONIN SCALIA: As long as there is licensing, I don't see how
we can stop wrestling with the basic problem of relations
between government and media. The government has to
determine who is the best licensee. Now, one of the most important obligations of a licensee is to be a responsible journalist; and to determine responsibility, you have to look at
the content of his news programs to see if it is balanced—has
the broadcaster generally made available all sides of controversial issues of public importance? In other words, as long
as you have government licensing, it is very difficult to get
away from some form of the Fairness Doctrine.

What the Office of Telecommunications Policy has proposed for the FCC to consider is that the Fairness Doctrine
be applied with much less stringency than in the past; that
the licensee's performance be evaluated at the end of his
license term when his renewal comes before the Commission;
and that the Commission just ask the broad question: Has
this fellow been a responsible journalist?

RICHARD SALANT: As I understand the First Amendment, it
says that nobody in government or elsewhere shall decide
that its protection goes only to the responsible and deserving
journalist and must be withheld from the irresponsible and

undeserving members of our trade. That is why I jump when Mr. Scalia says that once every three years, or once every five years, the government should ask: Has this broadcaster been a responsible journalist? This means that the government must decide whether a broadcaster should continue to exist—because licensing is a matter of life and death; not a fine, not a jail sentence, but a matter of survival. For the government to decide that a journalistic enterprise should or should not exist on the basis of an official judgment of responsibility—well, that might be all right if my friends are going to make the decision, but my friends are never in government. All I want to know is: Does the First Amendment apply to me, and if not, why not?

SCALIA: Consequences are bound to follow from licensing once you have a system in which you attempt to give the license to the person who does the best job. If you want to give the license by drawing lots or auctioning it off to the highest bidder, you could get away from the criterion of who will do the best job. But if you go that route, you would have to argue that it is better to have incompetent and irresponsible licensees than to risk infringing upon the First Amendment by permitting the government to look over the shoulder of a broadcaster.

NEWTON MINOW: When I first went to the Federal Communications Commission, and joined all those who have tried to figure out what the law meant, I found that the man who actually wrote the enabling act, Senator Dill from the state of Washington, was still alive. I tracked him down and asked him how he reconciled the conflict between the ban on censorship and the requirement that the broadcaster meet a statutory standard of "public interest, convenience, and necessity." The Senator said, "Well, young man when we were writing that law, we knew we had to have some kind of a standard, and I had a young lawyer working for me who had been at the Interstate Commerce Commission where they regulated public utilities and railroads, and the statutory standard of the Interstate Commerce Act was the public interest, convenience, and necessity. That sounded pretty good, and we couldn't think of anything else, so we put it in the Federal Communications Act."

Now, that decision of about forty years ago is why we are here talking about this problem today. The statutory standard, which is as broad as the language of the general welfare clause in the Constitution, is imposed in an Act of Congress, which at the same time says broadcasting is not a public utility and, further, that the government is not to censor what a broadcaster broadcasts.

HARRY KALVEN, JR.: One of the odd things is how little advice the Constitution has been able to give us on the problems raised by the advent of broadcasting. I am in the middle of trying to write a book about the First Amendment, and I find that the courts had about four hundred occasions in the last fifty years to work out the meaning of the Amendment as applied to other, older communications media. It has been an elegant judicial process, a kind of Socratic dialogue in which a new problem arises in a case that is a little different from those already agreed upon, and so we constantly have been provided with a filled-in answer to what the Amendment means for the print media. The courts' total performance here is most impressive.

In all this, broadcasting really has been slighted. A conventional casebook will not have anything in it about the broadcasting problem. The *Red Lion* case may rate a footnote, but until that decision came down, there was simply nothing you could turn to. There was no case that actually represented any considered judgment by the courts about the application of the First Amendment to broadcasting. And *Red Lion* is, as I think most of you know, curiously unhelpful—I was one of the losing lawyers in the case, so I am entitled to say so. Here was a great chance for the Supreme Court to say something definitive in answer to Mr. Salant's question, but all we got was a very crabbed, very fragile precedent that deals only with a limited application of the personal attack aspect of the Fairness Doctrine.

I think the First Amendment undoubtedly does, in some sense, apply to broadcasting. That is a very unhelpful answer, however, because the degree to which it controls is entirely an open question at this point.

LAWRENCE H. ROGERS II: Mr. Kalven seems to be suggesting that the imperfection of law on the subject is the fault of the licensees for not having brought more cases to court. I suggest that one reason for that is that we station owners have been too busy fighting off bureaucratic and administrative regulation by FCC. As I remember *Red Lion,* it was a unanimous decision of the Supreme Court. If that decision is not to be the law for all the rest of our natural lives, how do we go about doing something about it?

PAUL PORTER: When the FCC was first set up, the chairman was accused of regulation by threat. Under his successor, there was regulation by what was called the elevated eyebrow. Then I succeeded to the chairmanship, and there was regulation by exposure—the promulgation of the famous *Blue Book* setting up broadcast standards which had about half the industry on temporary license. After Porter there came a period of relative quiescence, until Newt Minow came along and practiced regulation by exhortation, pointing to that vast wasteland of TV programming. Today there are many commentators who feel that we are again up against an attempt at regulation by threat and intimidation.

Now, I contend that the court decisions in this area are narrowly based on a scarcity doctrine that no longer applies. We have the technological sophistication to provide all the channels anybody can use. So why not give broadcasters permanent licenses, and hold them responsible in the market-place? I came to this view after long experience with efforts to make the broadcasters behave. When this gadget was invented, somebody had the foresight to attach a little thing that you can work with your finger and your thumb to turn it off or on. That guarantees consumer acceptance, and that ought to be the greatest deterrent to irresponsibility. So I say, let's forget the old cliché that the airways belong to the public and stop using regulation as a club. Let's let the marketplace decide. That's where you'll get the best decisions, and also protect any vestiges that may be left of the First Amendment.

Minow: But it's not that simple. When we ask, Does the First Amendment apply to broadcasting? I don't think we can answer the question if we stop with the interest of the licensee. Does it apply to the listener who supposedly has a right to hear? To a man who can't buy air time? The theory that we have followed since broadcasting was new is that it is a risky business, so we didn't want to regulate it as a public utility because we wanted to hold out the prospect of making money so that private investors would come in and develop a new communications system with private capital. That has been accomplished, but in the process the question has got very tangled because there are various people who want to say the First Amendment applies to me but doesn't apply to the other fellow. That is what the argument is about.

REUVEN FRANK: Isn't that falling into Dick Salant's trap? Is the First Amendment simple or not? Does it apply to everybody, or does it keep the government out of news dissemination? And if these other parties have an interest, is that a First Amendment interest? That is the question.

SCALIA: Maybe this is a strict constructionist approach, but I don't think the First Amendment does apply to the private broadcaster's restriction of free speech by denying certain views or certain persons access to his facilities. At that point we're beginning to talk about not how the First Amendment applies but rather whether it ought to apply, whether we ought to have a First Amendment. Is it not clear to everybody that these questions that we've been kicking around have no answer—whether CBS is biased on the liberal side or on the conservative side, whether NBC is giving sufficient weight to one view or to another view, whether ABC is talking about the most important issues? I think Vice-President Agnew is entitled to his opinion, and I think [FCC Commissioner] Nick Johnson is entitled to his, and everybody is entitled to disagree with both—that, I take it, is the point of the First Amendment. It is essentially an expression of profound skepticism, if not cynicism, about the ability of intelligent men to make judgments like these, and what the Amendment says is that government simply should not ask such questions. Now, maybe we're no longer that skeptical, maybe we now believe that we can sit back and say this is fair and this is unfair. If that is the case, then let's talk about what we're really talking about. Maybe we should get rid of the First Amendment, and let the government decide what the broadcasters should broadcast. I myself think that would be a terrible resolution, but it is really what we are discussing.

HARRY S. ASHMORE: It seems to me you have a built-in problem in the practical situation that exists in terms of effective national media. I certainly don't agree that there is an ideological monopoly, but in fact there are only a very limited number of national news organizations. Three networks provide truly national and international coverage; only they among broadcasters have the finances and the manpower to do an effective job. A few newspapers, the *New York Times* and the combination of the *Washington Post* and the *Los Angeles Times,* perhaps the *Wall Street Journal* in its specialized fashion, and a couple of news magazines are in the same league—and that's about all the national media we have. I dismiss the two wire services on the ground that they have a low common denominator that they have to satisfy and inherently are not capable of doing any kind of deep-probing investigative reporting. It follows, then, that if those few national news-gathering organizations are crippled or intimidated we can't expect a local teakettle radio station to do much for us in the way of news and public affairs.

PORTER: I would take a dissent from that. I do a great deal of traveling. News is what I look at, and I turn on the television set in Dallas or in Oklahoma City, and I'm constantly amazed at the ingenuity of the local news organizations that precede the network news.

ASHMORE: You are talking about local coverage. I'm talking

about national coverage. No local television station can cover Washington and London and Saigon—which also means it can't do an investigative job on such a story as the Watergate case.

PORTER: Doesn't that take you into an economic issue? I asked the three network representatives here today whether their revenues solely attributable to network news and public affairs covered the costs of their news organizations, and the answer is uniformly no. This is their loss leader—and it is also the thing they do best.

ASHMORE: I understand that, and that is the reason we have had a decline in documentaries, which I count among the most valuable journalistic developments of our time. White-head's proposal would reduce the independence of these national news-gathering organizations and transfer the ultimate news judgment to local stations. The networks, as wholesalers of national and international news to the local stations, are in a situation that may be fundamentally different from any that applies across the board to all media outlets.

ROGERS: I have entertained Whitehead for a colloquy with my corporate colleagues, and I cannot agree with your characterization of his rhetoric. He never implied that the efficacy or the performance of the networks should be reduced in any way. What he did was repeat a truism that has been inherent in the Communications Act since 1934, that in accepting the line-up of news from a network a local station was not relieved from its over-all obligation to provide all shades of opinion. Specifically he said that if in the opinion of a licensee its particular network played the news in a way that was not to the satisfaction of the licensee, then it was the licensee's responsibility to supply whatever missing information or counter-information was needed to supply balance. Now, this is a vastly different thing from attacking either the credibility or the efficiency of the network news organizations. . . .

ASHMORE: But in his public statements that is precisely what Whitehead has done—couple his insistence upon local control with condemnation of the networks for lack of integrity.

ROGERS: The important thing is that if by government fiat or some other happenstance networks ceased to exist tomorrow, in meeting my responsibility to my stockholders I would have to get together with other stations in all parts of the country and invent something to replace them. Networks are really the product of the need of local stations to provide that which it is utterly impossible economically to provide on a local basis. A network is a co-op, and if it is an unsuccessful co-op it will fail.

SCALIA: I would like to second the explanation that Whitehead didn't call for anything except what is in the Communications Act. The Act places the responsibility on individual station owners to come up with programming that meets the public interest, convenience, and necessity. All Mr. Whitehead has done is to underline that responsibility.

SALANT: I would like to ask the defenders of Commander Whitehead what would happen if a local station at the time of its renewal announced that it thought the network news was fair, objective, and unbiased, and that it didn't propose to do a damned thing about it.

SCALIA: I can't speak for Whitehead, but I presume from what he said that if that was a judgment arrived at by the local station owner honestly, in good faith, and in accordance with his responsibilities under the Act, so be it.

SALANT: Who tests the honesty and good faith?

SCALIA: Not Whitehead.

SALANT: It seems to me that if we are going to get into a discussion of what Whitehead said and meant, one has to assume that he had something in mind—he wasn't just trying to fill up half an hour of time before Sigma Delta Chi in Indianapolis. One has to assume that he was trying to persuade somebody to do something. Now, if he was simply trying to persuade the network affiliates to start looking at the broadcasts that come down the line, then he is terribly naïve, because all one has to do is look at the communications we get to know that we hear from them constantly. They are always beefing about something.

SCALIA: It isn't beefing about them that the Act requires, it is making a judgment as to the coverage of all serious controversial matters and balancing whatever they think is unbalanced.

SALANT: It seems to me fairly clear that Whitehead, in coupling what he said about five-year licenses and so on with an explicit attack on network news, was telling the affiliates to do something about it. Now, if he had left out the Buchanan language about ideological payola, whatever that means . . .

SCALIA: Look, are you here to criticize Whitehead's proposals or his speech writing? I mean, if it is infelicitous phrases you are concerned with, you know, we can talk about that. I'm talking about his proposals.

PORTER: I am looking at the proposed statute right now. I don't think it changes the Act a hell of a lot.

SCALIA: I think it changes it—but the only respect in which it does change it is to provide more leeway and less government control. What Whitehead is suggesting is the elimination of program category criteria that the FCC now uses. You should have such-and-such a percentage of entertainment, such-and-such a percentage of farm programming, such-and-such a percentage of this, that, and the other. The proposals are a move in the opposite direction from more government control.

RICK J. CARLSON: Aren't we demonstrating the deviation from First Amendment philosophy by this discussion? It seems clear to me that what this administration has done is to decide that among the media it's constituency lies at the licensee level and not at the network level. Four, eight years from now, another administration may decide that its constituency lies at the network level and not at the licensee level, and roll back whatever legislation may be passed. That is exactly the danger the First Amendment speaks to: indirect influence by government—whatever the political stripe may be—on the dissemination of news.

ERIC SEVAREID: Isn't it fair to say that the thrust of the

Whitehead campaign is an attempt not at direct censorship, but to impose self-censorship?

SCALIA: Well, you know, one man's self-censorship is another man's editorial responsibility. If all you mean by self-censorship is that the station owner has to meet his responsibility to be a responsible broadcaster . . .

SEVAREID: But the test is criteria determined by government. What the whole argument is about, as I see it, is whether the government should pass on program content in any way whatsoever—whether you would allow censorship in through one alley or another.

SCALIA: The Whitehead proposal moves the government a step back, if you look at the proposal. What you are arguing against is not the Whitehead proposal but the Federal Communications Act, which now provides every restriction that the Whitehead proposal applies, and something more which he proposes to eliminate.

SEVAREID: I don't think it will move the government back. I think that in simple, practical terms the local stations would be encouraged to break up network programs as such, and make us over into an AP or UPI news service so the local station can throw out me or some other fellow, put in somebody of its own choice, put its own thing together, sell it, maybe make more money that way. Well, it would be different. I am sure we couldn't afford to do a lot of tough, expensive investigative reporting if acceptance by the local stations was very, very speculative. I think that is really what the administration wants to see happen.

BLAIR CLARK: I want to ask Mr. Scalia what has happened in the last few years that makes the Whitehead proposal applicable. Were these problems always there, waiting to be discovered by a new administration? Or are there philosophic underpinnings to this proposal? Finally, I would ask him to deal with the question of the threatening quality of these proposals to what I consider to be the freedom of broadcasting.

SCALIA: Well, first let me make it clear again that everything I say is not on Whitehead's behalf, or on the administration's behalf. I was not at OTP when the latest proposals were issued, but I would imagine that what lies behind them is a genuine belief that the industry is overregulated, that the government is too much involved in the media. The latest bill that Whitehead proposed is of the same cut. Whatever regulatory features it has exist under the current law.

PORTER: If I understand you, you are equating this new proposal with a sort of emancipation proclamation for the broadcast industry.

SCALIA: I would not go that far.

ASHMORE: It seems odd that those being emancipated see it as the reverse.

FRANK: We have heard a lot about what Whitehead said in his speech in Indianapolis, and in his various interviews, but the draft law Paul Porter was quoting doesn't include the worst of his strictures. I think it is worth quoting the speech, the Indianapolis speech, quite apart from the Act, and here is a paragraph that I find interesting: "Station managers and network officials who fail to act to correct imbalance of consistent bias from the networks, or who acquiesce by silence, can only be considered willing participants to be held fully accountable by the broadcasters' community at license renewal time."

Now, that, in the wonderful way that people have been developing lately of putting subjective considerations into objective-sounding words, means you do what we like or you are out of business. From a station's point of view a case could be made that if it didn't carry anything controversial from the network, it would be home free. You could postulate that imbalance or consistent bias would mean one thing to Mr. Whitehead, and something else to the man who would have sat in the Office of Telecommunications Policy had the election last November gone the other way, or to the people now being appointed to the FCC, and the people who would have been appointed by George McGovern. Whitehead may indeed mean to establish fewer restrictions on news broadcasting, but I can't see how it is going to end up that way. That's giving him the best of it.

ROGERS: Reuven, I have to respond by saying that if we all get together and pass this bill with a five-year license renewal, we know perfectly well Whitehead and Nixon won't be there the next time we have renewals, and that is one reason for doing it.

DONALD McDONALD: Mr. Whitehead speaks, maybe not with a forked tongue, but with ambiguity when he talks with one group or another. It's ingenuous to suggest that what the new bill is going to do is to withdraw the government when it leaves ultimate authority where it is, to be exercised by the government.

ROGERS: Well, this gets back to my original point that I don't know why everybody is so excited, because no White House spokesman, regardless of his title, has the power to impose this kind of regulation until the law is amended. That power is in Congress, it is not in the White House.

SALANT: That phrase in the Whitehead bill about considering the community is intended to be read in relation to the question of news and journalism. That frightens me even more. I believe any editor would agree that it is a terrible way to run a newspaper, to go into the community and find out what the customers want to hear and what they don't want to hear. You can't handle news on that basis. That's the iniquity of it.

SCALIA: Oh, you are trying hard to read it that way.

SALANT: I'm not trying hard. I would much rather sleep well at night.

SCALIA: No, I don't think it is meant that way at all. I think it probably does indicate that in some communities more news and public affairs may be desired than in others, and if a licensee is not providing to that community more than what comes down the pipe from the network, that licensee better do it, but I don't think it means that he only has to give them the kind of news they want to hear. I think . . .

ASHMORE: What does Mr. Whitehead mean when he says

that license renewal will depend upon the applicant having, quote: "demonstrated that he has been substantially in tune with the needs and interests of the community concerned"? Can a network be said to be protected by the First Amendment if its news judgment can be tested by a government agency on that basis?

SALANT: That is why I say we do need some sort of protection, if only because of the state of mind that is created by what people in government say, rather than by what the government actually does to us directly. We think we can take care of direct pressure as well as people in the print media do. When Dan Schorr gets ordered into the White House for a scolding, he can take care of himself, because he knows I'm not going to knuckle under. When John Ehrlichman asked me to breakfast and suggested, not facetiously, that Dan Rather be assigned back to his beat in Texas—which he never had—Ehrlichman could be assured that that guaranteed Dan Rather's having the White House beat as long as Dan Rather wants it, for the rest of his life if he chooses. What we need is protection against the kind of indirect pressure we interpret the Whitehead speech to foster.

We have talked about Whitehead's apparent desire to use the stations as a lever against the networks. Now, whether it's true or not, that's the way many of us perceive it. It is consistent with the pattern that has been established by Herb Klein [White House communications director], who went out to the National Association of Broadcasters and said, "What do you need the networks for?" and so on and so on. You can see a number of stations already buying insurance for that tempting five-year license renewal by writing me to tell me how awful our news broadcasts are. We need protection on this front, some sort of assurance that the government can't get too far into our program content by this back-door route. People have ignored the second part of the Whitehead speech, which is the other, equally dangerous side of the pincers movement. He said that the networks could retain their licenses—and it is nonsense to say that we are not licensed, because the network cannot survive without the revenue from the stations it owns, so for all practical purposes we are under the licensing gun—and Whitehead is saying that these stations can't maintain their licenses unless top CBS management stops saying that their news organizations have to be independent of the station management. This simply guarantees that our newsrooms will be inundated by two groups of people who have absolutely no right to be there—one, the affiliates, and two, the network bosses.

We can already measure the result. I don't get complaints about our broadcasts from high government officials any more. When I got such a call, some years back, complaining about a broadcast that had just gone off the air, I told the caller that I found that very interesting, and that any further calls I received from him would be on the record. I have never got a White House call since. But high government officials call up my bosses. It's my bosses who have the licenses, it's my bosses who have the greatest stake in getting them renewed, and my bosses are understandably nervous.

Now, I don't know how you can provide protection against this sort of intervention short of devising something which will define, once and for all, as we thought the First Amendment did, what the government can do in terms of oversight of content of news broadcasts. I think we waste our time talking about permanent licenses, simply because they are not politically feasible. Besides, I'm not sure everybody deserves a permanent license. But I don't think it is beyond our ingenuity to devise what I once called a Bill of Rights for broadcasting—draw up a legal ruling that says to the government you can go this far and no farther. On a temporary basis, to see how it works, I would like to see a simple amendment to the Communications Act saying that in granting, renewing, or revoking licenses, the content of news broadcasts shall not be taken into consideration.

ASHMORE: How could you have a Fairness Doctrine without taking into account the content of the broadcast?

SALANT: You couldn't.

ASHMORE: Well, now, the Fairness Doctrine seems to me to almost fit your prescription—what you had in mind when you said you thought proper action by the government would be to draw some kind of line and say this is where we think your First Amendment protection stops. Doesn't the FCC say, in effect, if you don't provide fair treatment on certain controversial issues, then we are going to have to intervene? I am not saying the Fairness Doctrine is drawn too well, but isn't that in principle what you are talking about?

SALANT: No, I don't think so. You see, you place me in a difficult position in arguing against the Fairness Doctrine, because it looks as though we are saying that we don't have to be fair. I deeply believe that the essence of professional journalism is fairness. The fact is that so far the Fairness Doctrine has given us no real problem except that it is a nuisance to respond to all these letters that the lawyers send to us. They make us go back and look at our records.

ASHMORE: But I understand you to be objecting to the present Fairness Doctrine in principle.

SALANT: No, I am not—no, no. I am not objecting to fairness as a principle. I am objecting to the fact that the power to decide whether we have been fair—that is, professional— resides in seven government officials, none of whom has any competence to make such a judgment. Even if they had such competence, I think it is a bad thing. What I am asking for as a broadcast journalist is precisely the same rights you had when you were editor of a newspaper—no more, no less. We want to be treated as professional journalists.

# CHAPTER 3

# THE ADVERSARY
# ROLE

THERE WAS general support for Richard Salant's contention that broadcasters require the First Amendment protections accorded the print media if they are to fully carry out their function as journalists. Under accepted tradition that role requires them to maintain, when necessary, an adversary relationship to government officials who may be assumed, in any administration, to be trying to use the media for self-serving ends.

The matter of scale came into the discussion here. The networks maintain what may well be the most effective of the few national news-gathering organizations staffed and financed in a fashion that permits intensive investigative reporting of national and international affairs. Any reduction of their capacity to deal with recalcitrant or importunate government officials from a position of independence would obviously affect the people's constitutional right to be informed about the conduct of public business.

The presidency carries with it the great advantage of incumbency, which permits the White House to command access to the media's communications facilities pretty much on the President's own terms. Thus he has an edge in advocating public policy, or defending his record of stewardship, that no combination of his formal political opponents can match. As J. William Fulbright, chairman of the Senate Foreign Relations Committee, has observed: "Whenever he wishes, [the President] can command a national television audience to hear his views on controversial matters in prime time, on short notice, at whatever length he chooses, and at no expense to the federal government or his party." The opportunity for rebuttal, if any, is usually limited to the Sunday-afternoon network interviews, described by Senator Fulbright as a modern, if less lethal, equivalent of the Roman arena: "Only when the interviewee happens to be the President of the United States is the usual Christian-and-lions format altered; on these uncommon occasions the reporters appear in the role of supplicants at Nero's court." It follows that any reduction in the broadcast journalist's ability to challenge presidential views or criticize presidential policy over the same communications channel will, as the *Washington Post* contends, strike at the very heart of the "First Amendment's notion that a people, in order to maintain their freedom, must know as much as possible about what their government is doing for or to them. . . ."

Restraints on Washington news coverage under the Nixon administration are the most stringent in modern times, and the President has continued to widen the scope of his claimed executive privilege to bar not only reporters but congressmen from access to key officials and documentary records. Nixon's remoteness from the White House press corps is bolstered by the outright hostility of his inner circle of advisers.

In this instance, broadcast journalists are not singled out; the tactics of evasion and retaliation apply equally to representatives of newspapers and magazines the White House considers unfriendly. Cases in which the administration or one of its agencies invokes the sanctions of law to harass newsmen by ordering them to testify in court or divulge records under subpoena are increasing, and presumably this may lead to clarification of the reach of the First Amendment in the cloudy area of conflict between judicial authority and press privilege. Members of both the Senate and House have gone into court to initiate action challenging the extent of executive privilege, launching a new line of litigation under the constitutional theory of division of powers.

The arrogance of the Nixon Administration in its dealings with Congress created an atmosphere on Capitol Hill in which the sparks of scandal from Watergate touched off a full-fledged constitutional conflagration. A stubborn district court judge and two persistent police reporters from the *Washington Post* appear to have been the primary instruments that headed off the effort to cover up the widespread campaign of espionage, sabotage, and intimidation mounted by the Committee to Re-elect the President with the connivance of key White House officials. The fallout was sufficient to insure the creation of a select Senate investigating committee under Sam J. Ervin, Jr., of North Carolina, and for the first time since Richard Nixon gained the White House the incumbent President lost the advantage in manipulating the media.

With witnesses testifying under oath and faced with penalties for perjury, interrogators beyond the long reach of the presidency were able to ask the hard questions that were ignored or dismissed at White House press briefings, and network cameras followed the initial hearings from gavel to gavel as Ervin and his colleagues laid bare a record that confirmed the most paranoid suspicions voiced by the participants at the Center conference. There could hardly have been a more dramatic demonstration of what the First Amendment is supposed to be about, and of how badly it has been abused.

As the Senate investigation began to probe into events preceding the burglary of the Democratic National Committee it became clear that this foray was only the tip of the iceberg. An "enemies list" containing the names of hundreds of persons nominated by White House staff members for special tax audits by the Internal Revenue Service embraced members of the Senate and the House (including all black congressmen), businessmen and educators who had differed with Nixon policies, and scores of newsmen. Some of these had the added distinction of having had their telephones bugged by the White House's electronic "plumbers."

Historian Henry Steele Commager saw the resort to secrecy as the prime cause of such "pervasive corruption" of the democratic process: "The assault on the Constitution—an assault which takes the form of the usurpation of executive authority, of the challenge to congressional control of the purse, and of the subversion of some of the most fundamental of our rights such as freedom of speech and of press, immunity from unlawful search, and the guarantee of due process of law—is perhaps the leading feature of the current political scene."

All the constitutional rights claimed on behalf of the media derive from the presumption that the constituency has the right to know what is going on at all levels of government, and that the right can be exercised on behalf of the public only by a communications system free of censorship or other governmental restraint. Alexis de Tocqueville expressed the prevailing view among the Founding Fathers when he wrote in *Democracy in America:* "The sovereignty of the people and the liberty of the press may be looked upon as correlative institutions."

Yet, as Rexford Guy Tugwell, the constitutional authority among the Center's Senior Fellows, has pointed out, the Constitution nowhere spells out the people's right to know. Drawing upon his own Washington experience as a cabinet officer and White House adviser in the days when Franklin Roosevelt had fun and played games in his relations with a nominally hostile press, Tugwell pointed out that there really are no effective guidelines to determine the limit of confidentiality, which everyone concedes must apply to some extent in the conduct of governmental affairs.

"This access to information the newsmen are demanding involves the whole business of confidential exchanges among officials, which clearly must be preserved to some extent if the government is to operate," Tugwell said. "A cabinet officer could no more formulate a policy and plan a program with a newsman looking over his shoulder than a newsman could carry out his function with a government censor scanning his output. The First Amendment, at least as it has been interpreted to date, provides no help in resolving this dilemma. In the name of national security or executive privilege everything the President and some thousands of other key officials may say or do can be classified and kept beyond access by the news media, and even by the congressional committees charged with oversight of specific governmental functions.

"Surely this constitutes a grave inhibition on the people's right to know—which I agree they do, and must have. But it is hardly an either/or question; some part of the official record must be confidential, at least temporarily. I doubt that we are going to work our way out of this dilemma without a constitutional amendment that defines a policy and places limits on its application."

In quieter times, when there was a higher degree of mutual confidence between public officials and representatives of the media, both sides tended to rely on the conscience of the other. In wartime the press was asked to voluntarily censor itself in areas where the government could not practically apply official restraints on information presumed to be helpful to the enemy. Turner Catledge, the retired executive editor of the *New York Times,* has observed that in the case of information involving troop movements, ship sailings, or imminent military plans, the question of censorship would never arise because the *Times* and any other responsible news medium would on its own motion refuse to reveal it.

In the celebrated case of the *Pentagon Papers,* in which for the first time in history the Department of Justice sought to establish a constitutional right to invoke prior restraint on publication, the editors of the *Times* undertook their own "balancing test" and decided that the public interest in having access to the documented background of official decision-making in the Vietnam war outweighed any possible aid and comfort its publication might provide the enemy. The Supreme Court majority agreed that the First Amendment gave the *Times* this discretion, but Mr. Nixon's appointees vigorously dissented—with Chief Justice Burger holding that the *Times* had no more right to use stolen government "property" for its own purposes than did a taxi driver who might find purloined matter in the back seat of his cab.

Catledge observed that "no one at the *Times* felt that we were *elected* to declassify the material. That's an obligation and a responsibility we voluntarily took on ourselves along with all the rest. But we felt, as the Court implicitly said, that the public interest is not served by classification and retention in secret of vast amounts of information. . . . The question of what constitutes national security and national interest was left undefined in the Court's decision and it is undefined anywhere else I know."

In another celebrated instance, *Times* editors tilted the

balance the other way, and decided to withhold information about the CIA's preparations for the abortive Bay of Pigs invasion of Cuba. Ten days before the operation began, the *Times* had in hand a dispatch filed from Miami by its Latin American expert, Tad Szulc, which documented the preparations going forward in Guatemala, established the CIA's role, and declared the invasion imminent. After much anguished conferring among the newspaper's top executives, including Orvil Dryfoos, then publisher, the Szulc dispatch was edited to remove the references to the CIA and to the imminence of the action.

Clifton Daniel, then managing editor of the *Times*, has provided an inside view of the incident and its aftermath. With the benefit of hindsight, he said, most of the *Times* principals came to believe they should have gone ahead with publication of the Szulc dispatch. And Daniel added this remarkable footnote in an account of a White House meeting of news executives called by President Kennedy two weeks after the Bay of Pigs fiasco to complain about press coverage:

"President Kennedy ran down a list of what he called premature disclosures of security information. His examples were drawn mainly from the *New York Times*. . . . Mr. Catledge pointed out that this information had been published in *La Hora* in Guatemala and in *The Nation* in this country before it was ever published in the *Times*.

" 'But it was not news until it appeared in the *Times*,' the President replied.

"While he scolded the *New York Times*, the President said in an aside to Mr. Catledge, 'If you had printed more about the operation, you would have saved us from a colossal mistake.' More than a year later, President Kennedy [told] Orvil Dryfoos, 'I wish you had run everything on Cuba. . . . I am just sorry you didn't tell it all at the time.' "

It would be hard to imagine that kind of interchange, with its confession of error and self-doubt on both sides, taking place in Richard Nixon's Washington. Instead, the press-rooms of the key government agencies have become battle-grounds where reporters, cast by conscience or circumstance in the traditional adversary role, find themselves confronted by public officials who not only evade the obligation to conduct public business in public but implicitly refuse to acknowledge that such an obligation exists. Here is how the issue was drawn at the Center conference:

HAROLD WILLENS: I think we have to begin with the fact that the media's function, as I believe Mr. Scalia agrees, is to develop and sustain an adversary relationship with government. But I happen to believe that this particular administration—perhaps also others before it, but I am particularly conscious of this one—does not really tolerate such an adversary relationship. Now, it's clear that big government can only be countered by powerful operations of some kind. Who else, for example, is capable of producing and disseminating a critical exposé like the Selling of the Pentagon? I don't even know if CBS would ever show that documentary again, in the wake of all the trouble it caused. Yet here is the Pentagon, a massive tapeworm which consumes an enormous amount of our money every year, and spends almost two hundred million dollars of that money in self-serving public relations. The Pentagon produces films and radio broadcasts, and so on, and makes them available all over the country to small stations. This is a highly effective marketing process, or propaganda campaign, intended to maintain and enlarge public support for the Pentagon's spending program.

What can possibly counter this kind of thing except a communications network strong enough and independent enough to produce something like the Selling of the Pentagon to let the citizenry know their tax money is being used in this propagandistic fashion? How can that kind of adversary message be sent out from Washington if the network news operations are fragmented in the fashion the administration is proposing?

SCALIA: I think you are just plain mistaken when you say that no adversary relationship can exist on the part of a small station. A little radio station is the most recent of the few stations to have its license revoked—Carl McIntyre's station in Maryland, which was vehemently critical of President Nixon and everything else. If you're looking for dissent, there was a station with plenty of dissent. It was essentially the Fairness Doctrine that sent it under. I am not proposing, and it's not my understanding that the administration is proposing, that there be no networks. Networks are a good and needed thing. In any case, CBS didn't carry the Selling of the Pentagon—it was broadcast only by its owned and operated stations in five major cities. . . .

WILLENS: Yes, but CBS had the guts and the money to produce it. And it took hell from the government after it did.

SCALIA: That's why networks are needed. Now, as for taking hell from the government, the point I was trying to make—

PORTER: That was television's finest hour.

SCALIA: The point I was trying to make is that I agree that the adversary relationship ought to exist. I would worry about the kind of a press we have in this country if it didn't exist. But, if you have an adversary relationship, you have to expect some give-and-take on both sides. The press, to my mind, is being excessively thin-skinned when it takes the kind of umbrage that it did at Vice-President Agnew's comments. I think the press ought to keep whacking at the government whenever it thinks it's wrong. But government officials ought to be able to come back and say so when they think the press is wrong, or is being irresponsible.

SALANT: I couldn't agree with you more, as long as you don't hold the licensing power . . .

SEVAREID: You have the power of subpoena, and it was used in the Selling of the Pentagon case. This is a wholly different thing from complaint and criticism. You want to do battle with us, but we haven't got your weapons.

ASHMORE: I want to get into the record at this point Eugene McCarthy's remark on Agnew. He said he agreed with everything the Vice-President said, but denied his right to say it.

SCALIA: I really think it is taking an irresponsible position to claim First Amendment privileges and then argue that government officials should not be allowed to defend their policies and to point out where they think the press has been irresponsible. As a matter of fact, every administration has done it, beginning with George Washington . . .

SALANT: But Agnew did more than complain. If you will go back and read those early speeches, you will see that he kept on reminding us that we were licensed.

McDONALD: And Dean Burch, the chairman of FCC, followed up the Agnew speech with requests for transcripts of the commentaries on a speech of Mr. Nixon's by the network commentators.

CLARK: There is implicit in what Mr. Whitehead says—and what Mr. Scalia says with a great deal more civility—the notion that the adversary relationship has to do with two parties operating more or less as equals. To argue that in the present case requires the assumption that the great power of the government is not a factor that necessarily underlies the statements of its spokesmen. It is extremely disingenuous to regard individuals in positions of great power as though they were private citizens defending themselves against the mass media. There is a touch of paranoia in maintaining that position when the government is inherently so much more powerful than the adversary with which it is dealing. The government makes the news, it regulates all parts of the apparatus required for the survival of broadcasting, and the notion that the two can be equated strikes me as false and deliberately misleading.

FRANK: By way of reminding you just how unequal that so-called adversary process is, I'd like to quote a colleague of mine who recently pointed out that there are many countries where politicians have taken power and put journalists in jail, but there is no country where journalists have taken power and put a politician in jail.

SCALIA: I think you are misinterpreting my endorsement of the existence of an adversary relationship. I mean there should be free and open debate, an adversary relationship at the level of public discussion, so that the Vice-President or any other governmental official, with the exception of those

—Dean Burch, for example—who are involved in the licensing process, all other government officials must be free to speak out. If the press can criticize the government in the interest of informing the public, surely government officials ought to be able to answer back. I think that's entirely proper. I do not think it's proper for the government to try to beat the press into the ground by any means other than persuasion and the making of intellectual points. That's the only adversary process I'm talking about.

KALVEN: I am grateful to Mr. Scalia for posing the question in a way which makes it possible to give a slogan answer. It's very plausible to suggest that any adversary relationship ought to go both ways. But I think in the case of the government and the press it should be a one-way adversary relationship. In a sense, the paradox of the First Amendment really is this: The lifeblood of First Amendment policy depends on criticism, but this depends upon a paramount prohibition which requires that the government cannot be the critic. There is no way the government can operate in this area as a polite critic, and a less-than-polite critic is bound to produce a chilling effect upon those being criticized. Therefore I think it makes more sense to say that this is a situation in which we have to lay symmetry to one side. The Constitution really does intend to guarantee one-way tension, through a one-way adversary system.

The notion of an asymmetric adversary relationship is novel, and Professor Kalven confessed after the conference ended that he was not altogether serious when he challenged Mr. Scalia's apparently sensible contention that the classic legal view of adversary procedure assumed a wide-open two-way exchange. Asked if, in the cold, sober light of aftermath, he wanted to stand by his thesis, Kalven found that he did, and replied with a brief essay under the title "If This Be Asymmetry, Make the Most of It!":

The "shock" of arguing for asymmetry captures by its very affront to sensible expectations the special quality of the American commitment to freedom of communication. It puts the preference for leaving the press alone more vividly, I think, than the phrase "preferred position," which provided so much of a constitutional battleground in the '40's. It suggests that the First Amendment involves not so much a meticulous prudential weighing of considerations between speech and censorship as it does a leap to commitment.

We can come at the point in various ways. It is an insufficiently noticed aspect of the First Amendment that it contemplates the vigorous use of self-help by the opponents of given doctrines, ideas, and political positions. It is not the theory that all ideas and positions are entitled to flourish under freedom of discussion. It is rather that they must survive and endure against hostile criticism. There is perhaps a paradox in that the suppression of speech by speech is part and parcel of the principle of freedom of speech. Indeed, one big reason why policy dictates that government keep its hands off communication is that in this area self-help of criticism is singularly effective.

"Who," asked Lord Ellenborough in 1808 in *Carr v. Hood*, a great English case on the privilege of fair comment in literary criticism, "would have bought the works of Robert Filmer after he had been refuted by Mr. Locke?" And this, of course, was the point of the famous Holmes reference to "the power of the thought to get itself accepted in the competition of the marketplace." And of the not quite so famous Brandeis observation that "the fitting remedy for evil counsels is good ones." The point then is that the First Amendment contemplates the unleashing of negative and destructive criticism against ideas and positions. There is just one condition, and it fits perfectly our asymmetry in adversaries: the government may not itself be the critic.

The asymmetry resonates on another major theme. I have argued that at the core of the First Amendment is the prohibition of seditious libel, of *the possibility* that the government or its officers can be defamed. This, as I read it, was the rationale of the great Supreme Court decision in *New York Times v. Sullivan* in 1964, which is the key to much modern development in constitutional law. "This is the lesson," Justice Brennan said, "to be drawn from the great controversy of the Sedition Act of 1798 . . . which first crystallized a national awareness of *the central meaning* of the First Amendment." Here, too, is the deliberate embracing of imbalance—the citizen-critic of government is placed pretty much beyond the reach of the sanction of defamation law.

What emerges then from reflections about the underlying rationale for freedom of speech seems to me quite congenial to the idea of deliberate asymmetry. Free, robust criticism of government, its officers and its policy, is the essence of the democratic dialectic, of "the belief," again to quote Brandeis, "in the power of reason as applied through public discussion." The government cannot reciprocally criticize the performance of the press, its officers, and its policies, without its criticism carrying implications of power and coercion. The government simply cannot be another discussant of the press's performance. Whether it will it or not, it is a critic who carries the threat of the censor—and more often than not, it wills it. Nor is it at all clear that its official voice will be needed; surely there will be others to champion its view of the performance of the press.

The balance struck then is avowedly, and even enthusiastically, one-sided. The citizen may criticize the performance and motives of his government. The government may defend its performance and its policies, but it may not criticize the performance and motives of its critics.

Perhaps the Nixon years make the appeal to asymmetry in adversaries especially attractive. They show how well nigh impossible it is for the government to criticize its critics without appearing to its critics, and to the public, to be intending to intimidate them. More important, the Nixon years show how difficult it is for the government to criticize the critics without appearing to question their right, and indeed obligation, to be critics. What seems to me to be singularly missing in the Nixon reaction to the press is any sense of acknowledgment that "robust,

uninhibited and wide open" debate on public issues and government policies is the American formula. And what has seemed
singularly missing in the emissaries of the Administration is any
sense of appetite for such debate.

The most elementary application of the Fairness Doctrine
clearly required that Antonin Scalia have a chance to reply
to these *ex post facto* reflections by Professor Kalven. A
member of the law faculty of the University of Virginia on
leave for service with the Nixon administration, Professor
Scalia entitled his rebuttal "The Most of It: Asymmetry Is
an Unbalanced View." Excerpts follow:

Like Professor Kalven, I am an aficionado of the paradox; and
I am thus aware of the dangers which attend that particular art
form. The intellectual fascination of linguistic sleight-of-hand
sometimes seduces one, for the sake of art, to overlook important
aspects of reality. Surely the "one-sided adversary relationship"
has had this siren effect on Professor Kalven, who otherwise sails
an exceedingly straight course. Since it was I who invented the
phrase (not as a paradox but as an absurdity) I feel some responsibility to prevent it from destroying still other fine minds.

The first reality which the "one-sided adversary relationship"
suppresses is the fact that the press itself is an exceedingly powerful institution in our society—more powerful, I think, than any
other except the government itself. In fact, as long as our democratic institutions are intact even the governmental power is
somewhat in thrall to the press, since it must rely upon that institution to present its views, its proposals, and its accomplish-
ments accurately and fairly to the electorate.

Quite properly, the only check we are willing to place upon
this powerful institution is criticism. But to be effective, that
criticism must be heard; to be heard it must appear in the press
itself; and to be sure of appearing in the press itself it must, in
some cases at least, be made by an "automatic newsmaker,"
that is, a high government official.

Dare to entertain for a moment, only for the sake of argument, the possibility that the Vice-President's criticism is true—that there exists a highly concentrated "national news" profession (in the television field at least, this hypothesis does not tax the imagination) and a non-conspiratorial but nonetheless real consensus among the members of that profession which results in a biased presentation of certain issues (which is surely arguable, for it has been heatedly argued). It should be apparent that the more truth such criticism contains, the less it can be expected to be given public prominence by the profession itself—not merely because human beings and associations of human beings rarely favor criticisms directed at themselves, but also because the very bias that is the object of the criticism would, if it existed, cause the criticism to be regarded as captious.

In fact, Vice-President Agnew's charges were not new; they had been vigorously made, by and within "conservative intellectual circles" (you doubtless think I am engaging my penchant for paradox) for several years. But the criticisms, unlike the alleged abuses at which they were directed, did not make the six o'clock news, and were not given the public attention that their importance warrants, until they were voiced by a high government official who could not be ignored.

If you find the example of the Vice-President's criticism of television news uncongenial and therefore unconvincing, substitute President Truman's criticism of the printed press. Whatever the rights or wrongs of the particular charges involved, I think it would be foolhardy to eliminate what is surely the most effective means, and may in some cases be the only means, of preserving the one check upon media power—press coverage of criticism of the press.

One might think it worth enduring this loss (though I personally would not agree) if the coercive power of the government itself were thereby significantly reduced. But here the principle of a "one-sided adversary relationship" ignores reality for the second time. It would muzzle government officials, and to that extent curtail public debate, because (in the words of its first convert) criticism "carries implications of power and coercion." But those implications can be made as easily without public criticism as with it, if the government is truly of a mind to abuse its power. In fact, it should be obvious that when improper threats are to be made or implied, the job is more naturally and more effectively done behind closed doors—and by non-government "spokesmen"—than in the glare of television cameras by the Vice-President.

In short, by curtailing public debate in the fashion suggested, the new principle would succeed in removing the one device *least* likely to be used as a means of improper coercion. It is for this reason that the national media's persistent attempts to portray the Vice-President's statements as a threat of improper exercise of government power are essentially unconvincing: The picture they paint makes as much sense as a rape in front of a police station. Even that portion of the public willing to grant the degree of evil intent that must be assumed cannot be convinced of the requisite degree of stupidity.

I rather suspect that if the press analyzed its own feelings it would find that it is smarting from no coercion except that which arises from the direction of public attention to serious criticisms, going to the heart of its professional responsibility, made for the first time in a fashion that required extensive coverage.

Finally, and most fundamental, the "one-sided adversary relationship," as a working principle, ignores the reality that government officials are flesh-and-blood human beings. While some of them may, with stern discipline, develop the self-control needed to refrain from commenting upon the judgment and ancestry of those who disapprove their daughters' singing, it is really too much to expect them to make no reference to what they regard as bias and incompetence on the part of those who publicly denounce their life's work. Such a code of conduct is designed not merely for another constitutional system, or another country, but for another world, inhabited by creatures who, I suspect, have five legs and antennae.

To demonstrate support for a theory of asymmetry in the doctrine of *New York Times v. Sullivan* is a task that could be successfully completed only by one who believes not merely in "one-sided adversary relationships" but also in square circles. One of the express rationales of that decision was the creation of *balance*, by according to private citizens who defame public officials something of the same privilege previously accorded public officials who defame private citizens in the course of their duties. In fact, to the extent an asymmetry remains, it favors the government, since the public official's privilege is absolute whereas the press or the private citizen must show good faith.

I have not said all that I might against the concept of the "one-sided adversary relationship." But since Professor Kalven's comments were short, I will not expand mine—even though I would maintain that he merely ran out of arguments while I ran out of space. As incomplete as this rebuttal may be, I am happy to present it because, being as I say addicted to paradox, I believe a job worth doing is worth doing badly.

I am inclined to award debater's points to both sides in this elegant exchange, but it does not resolve the basic issue. Professor Kalven contends that the imbalance of power between government and media is inherently so great it imposes an insurmountable handicap on the weaker adversary; Professor Scalia concedes that the media's power is second to that of government, but goes on to argue his case as though this disparity did not matter.

No one, certainly, denies the government's right to challenge the facts as presented by the media, and I would further concede that any aggrieved government spokesman is entitled to use the media for that purpose. Beyond that limit, however, lies the right of the two parties to indulge in criticism of the other's performance and motives, which cannot be limited to matters of factual accuracy.

It is here that Professor Kalven makes his claim for asymmetry. It rests upon the proposition that when a journalist criticizes the performance and motives of government he has shot his bolt; if the public rejects or discounts the charge, there is nothing more he can do about it, and he has run the considerable risk of personal damage in terms of lost credibility. On the other hand, if the government criticizes the performance and motives of the media, it is virtually bound to use its considerable powers to correct such derelictions against the common good—or at least leave its adversary under the impression that it may do so.

When a moderate "new Agnew" emerged in the wake of Watergate, the *New York Times* observed: "When a private citizen, no matter how wealthy or powerful, argues with the President or the Vice-President or a White House spokesman, it is not an argument between equals. The record of this Administration impels newsmen to regard its intentions with wariness and distrust. That is not paranoia; it is common sense. When the Vice-President's new verbal self-restraint is matched by the Administration's restraint in the exercise of its power, and not until then, the tradition of friendly adversaries may be restored."

Even that is too much for Professor Kalven. In his view the notion of a *friendly* adversary relationship evades the central point. "The government is entitled to a *loyal* opposition," he contends, "but the press is not to be confronted by even a friendly adversary in the form of government."

This splendid logic-chopping is, I think, useful and revealing—although, even if we gave the palm to Professor Kalven, we clearly would not be at the end of the argument. There would still remain the troublesome matter of agreeing upon a definition of *loyal* opposition.

# CHAPTER 4

# THE RIGHT
# OF ACCESS

A GOOD MANY of those who are willing to concede the theoretical right of broadcasters to function free of government intervention are not comfortable with the alternative of a private communications system whose owners and managers are constrained only by the market-place. The broadcasters themselves are ambivalent on the central issue of licensing. While they chafe under the restraints of FCC regulation, station owners have to recognize that the economic underpinning of their industry creates a considerable vested interest in maintaining a system more or less frozen into place by virtue of federal regulatory practices.

Lawrence Rogers recalled that in the early days of radio and TV the major newspapers displayed a singular indifference to the free marketplace when they rushed forward to acquire broadcast licenses. "I can tell you flatly out of my own experience," he said, "that the acquisition of these franchises by the publishers was not eleemosynary. It was for the specific purpose of keeping an upstart competitor under control so that it would not have an adverse effect on newspaper advertising rates."

Newton Minow observed that when the FCC opened up the UHF frequency band to provide more TV outlets, the existing VHF licensees bitterly opposed the move: "I told them they faced a choice between more competition and more regulation, and urged them to opt for competition—but they held out for keeping down the number of channels as long as they could."

Antonin Scalia noted that those already on deck were ready to repel boarders in the more recent case of the new cable systems: "They do not broadcast over the air, so there is no engineering justification for cable systems' being licensed, and the channels are so plentiful there is no scarcity issue. But the cable companies are being licensed by FCC just the same, in response to the broadcasters' demands that their potential competitors ought to at least suffer equal mistreatment."

The limitation on the number of licensed broadcasters accounts for the high profits returned to station owners from comparatively modest initial investments in equipment and operating costs. The result is that single stations in a major market, whose primary asset is the license for which the government makes no charge, have been sold for $50 million and up. "When you've got advertisers who will pay $200,000 for a minute's commercial on a Superbowl broadcast you've got economic scarcity, resulting in the desire of a lot of people to go into the broadcasting business," Minow said. "Broadcasting can return a financial bonanza, while no brave communicator wants to go into the newspaper business where, except in a monopoly market, the owner faces economic disaster."

The scarcity which guarantees the broadcaster's profits

also provides the rationale for the FCC's Fairness Doctrine. Here there has emerged a concept of public access that has not turned up in previous First Amendment controversies. In the case of electioneering politicians, the FCC some years ago ruled that if a station gives or sells time to one candidate it must make available equal time for his opponents on the same basis. This principle, broadened into the Fairness Doctrine, and upheld by the courts, now holds that broadcasters are obliged to present all sides on all issues of public controversy. While it does not guarantee any individual the right to address the broadcasters' audience, it greatly strengthens the hand of those who contend that their point of view is not fairly represented in the presentation of news and public affairs programming.

The argument that citizens have a right of access to the media under the First Amendment is recent, and has not yet been dealt with head-on by the courts. In 1967 a Harvard law professor, Jerome A. Barron, propounded the new theory in the *Harvard Law Review*, contending that freedom of the press has been reduced to an arbitrary protection for the owners of the media, a group whose number is steadily dwindling owing to technological and economic trends. The Supreme Court's decision in *Times vs. Sullivan*, which virtually repealed the law of libel, in Barron's view reinforced his argument that an individual or group aggrieved by a public personal attack needs some comparable legal recourse to guarantee right of reply on equal terms. The FCC in effect has established that principle in the case of broadcast calumny, and in *Red Lion* the Supreme Court sustained it.

In a background paper for the Center conference, Rick Carlson predicted that this novel legal concept of right of access would provide the cutting edge in future adjudication of the First Amendment. He noted that there are four

parties to the debate over the application of First Amendment rights: the government, the media, private individuals
and groups, and the undifferentiated public. The Supreme
Court, he said, had examined some of the interests of some
of these parties some of the time, but had not yet undertaken
to consider them as a whole. That, he predicted, is the
direction in which the Court is likely to move in response
to the growing tension among the several parties.

It is in the name of fairness that the Nixon administration
has attacked the media. The immediate threat the networks
read into Whitehead's strictures lies in the proposed application of the Fairness Doctrine to determine the balance of
programming in terms of local tastes and prejudices. But,
increasingly, broadcasters also are encountering new popular
pressures under the theory of public access. The political
left, while agreeing that the government should not intervene in program content, generally challenges the right of
private corporate owners to determine by their own lights
what should go on the air. Radical groups point out that
truly dissident views run counter to the self-interest of a
communications system wholly dependent upon advertising
revenue, which in turn is dependent upon high audience
ratings. The result is an inherent bias toward the status quo,
and a powerful tendency to avoid the kind of controversy
that attends significant social change. With considerable success, both right and left are fomenting what amounts to
populist pressures against the media. An eloquent example
of the case at its extreme can be seen in these excerpts from a
paper prepared for the conference by Visiting Fellow Ronald
Segal, expatriate South African social critic, under the title
"Whose Firebell in the Night?":

There are few spectacles less elating than that of a privately
owned communications industry tumescent with the self-righ-

teous indignation that any serious criticism of its prerogatives excites. Alarm bells are rung at the violence intended to the liberties of the citizen, until it seems that only the inalienable right of a few proprietors, individual or corporate, to market news and opinions, stands between democracy and the police state. And yet, surely, it is plain that the private ownership of mass communications must be a profound denial of the free society. That it is traditionally associated with liberalism is not a reason to continue conceding its necessity, but rather to question the value of traditional liberalism itself.

It cannot be that citizens are equally free in any state where a few command the virtually exclusive means to collect, refine, and disseminate news and opinions. To be sure, as is asserted in reply, anyone is free to establish competitive means; but, as everyone knows, the capital costs of doing so effectively are such as to add insult to injury by the assertion.

The proprietors, whether with the enthusiastic or with the cynical collaboration of those they employ, tend to provide a product that will promote the sort of society which sustains their proprietorship. And the developed dynamic of the market place is leading in mass communications, as in other industries, to concentration of control.

None of this is to suggest, however, that the current assault on the mass communications industry by the Nixon administration should be met with anything but alarm. For it is an assault on the liberal society in the cause not of more, but of less liberty. Indeed, taken together with the increasing imperiousness of presidential conduct it provides a forcible confirmation of the movement to authoritarianism.

This movement has a gathering popular appeal. It feeds on fear: of inflation, among those whose standards and security are being eroded; of a black irruption into their suburbs and schools, among those whose economic hold and social standing are uncertain; of the increase in crime and violence and ideological revolt; of the new world which the United States seems no longer to dominate, financially or militarily, as so recently it did; of an intricate technological society which treats people as the objects of processes beyond their comprehension and control.

What is needed is a truly liberating, essentially democratic alternative that offers people the possibilities of an equal participation in controlling the quality of their lives. It is appropriate here to consider only mass communications. And it must be clear that if private ownership should be discarded, so also should state ownership. For this last merely substitutes the vested interest of the particular government and its appointed bureaucracy for that of private management, while adding the formidable force of the state.

One must begin by discarding altogether the abstract, depersonalizing concept of the "public" and place in its stead the concrete existence of the "person." Why should not people own and control mass communications as directly as possible? In small town or city, they might provide special councils to manage the press, radio, and television, with members chosen either by lot from among all citizens, or by both lot and secret ballot.

Because as many citizens as possible should at some time in their lives exercise the responsibility of management, for the growth as well as the health of the democracy, membership of any such council for mass communications should be limited to a single year, and should disqualify the member from ever serving in the same capacity again. And because no majority should be allowed to monopolize the mass means of communicating opinion, individual citizens should be entitled to such space in the press or such time on radio and television as their numbers proportionately merit.

It will be asserted that mass communications are too complex and important for their management to be left to ordinary people. But this is essentially another way of saying that politics has become too complex and important an operation for ordinary people to manage. And if such is truly the assertion of liberalism, then those who assert it should scarcely be surprised, let alone indignant, at the moves of those who would place politics and mass communications connectedly in the keeping of the state: where ordinary people cannot reach to do themselves harm, or any good.

Attack and defense of Segal's thesis, and the objections he had anticipated as to its practicality, provided a leitmotiv for the remainder of the conference.

WENDELL MORDY: We haven't given as much attention as we should to the differences in kind in the media, for these have great bearing on the processes we are talking about. We all recognize essential differences between broadcasting and press. Broadcasting is more immediate, it is time-structured, and it touches all ages in a way that print media do not. Moreover, it provides a means of concentrating power which I think has never been characteristic of the newspaper press.

We have dealt with the need for another power focus to offset government power, and I am drawn to this argument. But I think we could develop an argument that the kind of power concentration now represented by broadcasting is inherently undemocratic. If this is the case—and I don't suggest that it necessarily is—then we are faced with a new problem that forces a different consideration of the matter of government regulation of broadcasting. When we talk about rights derived from freedom of speech, we have to take into account the fact that this particular medium allows fewer and fewer to talk to more and more. I think that inherently has an undemocratic element in it.

McDONALD: In his legal analysis of the First Amendment controversy Rick Carlson suggested that four parties are involved—private interests, public interests, the government, and the media. The broadcasters seem to be arguing that this is a private quarrel between two parties—the media and the government.

FRANK: I'd like to pursue that point with the legal experts. Before broadcasting came along, was there ever a First Amendment case that did not involve the act of publication? In other words, was there ever any other party to the litigation besides the government and the publisher when the case involved the dissemination of information?

KALVEN: I suppose not. The theory has been that the right to speak and the right to hear absolutely cohere. The public interest in having the benefit of public discussion on public issues is the predicate behind all First Amendment applications. The Constitution protects the individual publisher against government censorship on behalf of the public's right to rational debate on public issues.

CARLSON: But I don't accept the premise that there is harmony, or nearly coextensive harmony between the media's right to speak and the public's right to hear.

KALVEN: I take it you are raising the public interest as separate from the media's interest in an effort to show that the two might diverge under some circumstances—and that you rather suspect we have reached that point of diversion. You are asking whether the prior predicate is still convincing—whether we can continue to rely on a private champion to debate the public issues.

PORTER: I would like to hear a bill of particulars on what views and what interests, what minority groups, do not enjoy access under the existing system.

MINOW: Okay, let's pursue Paul's point. We're in a room here with a lot of microphones; each of us has access to a microphone. But there are some people out there who don't have such access. They can still speak. They have a First Amendment right to speak, but the people to whom these microphones are attuned are not going to hear them. The point is that the new demand is not access to media as such, it is access to the audience the media attract. You don't satisfy that demand by letting a dissident go on the air early on Sunday morning when the views he is protesting were aired on prime time.

PORTER: I would like to ask Mr. Willens about a case in point. You initiated an action in the courts in which your business-men's organization brought suit against the networks for refusing to sell you time to run a documentary setting forth your views on Vietnam. Didn't your organization's position on Vietnam get exposure on television news?

WILLENS: It was given considerable exposure, but we never felt that it was sufficient to balance the opposite view. We felt particularly that economic arguments were being ne-glected, arguments the business community could make to show that the Vietnam war was a fiasco, that in fact it was responsible for a spiral of inflation which would cost this country untold billions of dollars for an untold period of time. It was our point that this aspect of the controversy was never stressed, and unless we could somehow find some sexy, hard-news peg—which is not that easy to find—we couldn't get attention on the news programs, and therefore the only way to argue our case was through a paid advertise-ment. I must say I was astonished to find that, with hard cash money in hand, we couldn't buy the time on any network to state what we felt was a legitimate point of view.

SEVAREID: Mr. Willens, you didn't have to buy time from CBS to get your views recognized on the air. I remember your Baltimore associate coming to see me a long time ago. I talked about this argument of yours on the air with a con-siderable audience.

WILLENS: Yes, there's no question about that.

SEVAREID: Also a great deal was written about this issue in the press. That raises an interesting question about what groups are presumed to be suppressed. How do you know about them to begin with, except through the press?

SALANT: Only part of this is relevant to the issue of the degree to which the First Amendment applies to broadcast journalism, and that part may be what underlay the decision of my associates to turn down Mr. Willens' bid to buy time. Network policy forbids putting on news or commentary not of its own origination. One reason is that it must be assumed, since most of the money belongs to people who hold rather conservative views, that there would be a terrible imbalance if the broadcasters adopted the policy of accepting editorial advertisements from anybody who could pay cash for air time. Then the Fairness Doctrine certainly would have to come in.

PORTER: I can remember when it did. In the 1936 Roosevelt-Landon campaign, the advertising firm of Blackett, Sample and Hummert was employed by Governor Landon as his advertising agency. Hill Blackett, who is alleged to have been the creator of the radio soap opera, called upon his skills to adapt this art form for political purposes. As I recall, the result went something like this: John and Mary want to get married, and they go to the licensing clerk, and the licensing clerk says: "John, do you know that you are assuming a debt of $1,850 when you get married?" John says, "No, I hadn't heard that." Well, the happy couple decide, because of this condition—which exists, of course, because Roosevelt hadn't balanced the federal budget—that they either have to live a life of sin or of chastity. The FCC threw that off the air, and held that political issues are much too important to be decided by the skills of warring dramatists.

SCALIA: How did the soap opera come out?

PORTER: The agency was renamed Blackett, Sample, Hummert, Maine and Vermont.

SALANT: This question can't really be dealt with in terms of the advertisement Mr. Willens submitted on behalf of a citizens' group, because that isn't the way it is going to happen most of the time. Consider the question in terms of the oil industry coming in with a major documentary proving the necessity for an increase in the oil-depletion allowance. Now how do you feel about it?

ASHMORE: It is the same question, isn't it?

SALANT: Sure, it is the same question, but I bet that most of you would give a different answer.

ASHMORE: But aren't you simply dismissing the issue of right of access, which is the question we have before us?

SEVAREID: Nobody ever said anybody had the right of access to the public prints unless they were interesting enough to deserve attention. If they are they'll get it. I contend that applies to broadcasting too.

MINOW: Are you sure? Let's consider a real honest-to-God case. One day Mrs. Eleanor Roosevelt called me and reported that a black preacher was running for Congress in Jackson,

Mississippi, and had complained to the FCC that he couldn't get on television, and that nothing had been done about his complaint. I checked, and, sure enough, somewhere in the bowels of the FCC there was a complaint. The Reverend Robert L. T. Smith, a bona fide candidate for Congress, attested that he wasn't asking for something for nothing, or claiming race discrimination, he just wanted to buy TV time to campaign against the incumbent, John Bell Williams, on the only TV station that served the congressional district.

SALANT: You're stacking the deck. . . .

MINOW: No, I simply want to put the question to you and then you decide what you would have done if you had been in my place as chairman of FCC. We checked with the Jackson station, and the station said, Well, Congressman Williams isn't buying any time and therefore we are not going to sell any time to this fellow because we're required to treat them both equally. I called in the FCC lawyers and asked, Can this be right? Can there be a total blackout on political debate in this fashion? And they said, Well, that's the law, all the law says is that if you sell or give time to one candidate, you have got to sell or give time to the other. I said that can't be right—and we called the station and asked the manager to explain how he was serving the public interest, convenience, and necessity by not carrying political discussion in his area. The station came back and said, Well, we'll put the Reverend Mr. Smith on. Now, was that an illegitimate exercise of the government's authority?

SCALIA: The right of access occupies a somewhat different status from the other First Amendment rights we're talking about. Access, the right to reach the public, is not part of the

First Amendment in and of itself. Suppose the English governor had told Tom Paine that he could go ahead and publish all he liked, but at the back of his pamphlets he would have to allow the governor's assistant to publish his views to guarantee that he had given the other side. That would have preserved Tom's right of free speech, but far from being an implementation of the First Amendment, it would have been just the opposite. You would have to consider it a restriction upon speech if in order to print a broadside Tom Paine had to present not only his own views but also those of someone arguing on the other side. The First Amendment does not require the government to enable everyone to reach the public at large, and to interpret it that way is to make it ridiculous.

However, when the government itself is responsible for a particular communications medium, it must let everybody use it on a non-discriminatory basis. That is where the right of access begins to come in. It enters into our discussion here because the courts, in proceedings involving Mr. Willens' case, and others, are beginning to consider that in effect the holder of a broadcasting license is in some sense government —that is, since the government is so much involved in his activities, the government itself is a responsible party, and therefore access has to be allowed on a non-discriminatory basis.

FRANK: Discussion of the right of access in these terms, at least in my experience, is a new development, and it gives a lot of us all kinds of funny feelings. Anybody who has spent any time earning his living in the news business knows that people who are involved in a news event, whether they are setting forth a special point of view or merely viewing the action from a single angle, are likely to be unsatisfied with reports that are put together by professionals who are trying to be fair and detached. For example, Mr. Willens says that his point of view was not put forward adequately by CBS, although Mr. Sevareid expressed it to perhaps twenty million people and undoubtedly did so quite eloquently. Then you move on from the right of access to what I now hear described as the right to be heard. At some point this progression becomes not only illogical but obscene. The right to be heard, if such exists, has to imply coercion, because the right to be heard means forcing someone to listen. And that, I suggest, represents the most dangerous direction we could move in.

ASHMORE: I would like to cite a statement of Whitehead's, which I take it represents his view of what the Communications Act now requires of the FCC, and that is "to guarantee reasonable, realistic, practical opportunities for the presentation and discussion of conflicting views on controversial issues." Now, it seems to me that the clear and unmistakable implication is that there is a guarantee of access, for ideas at least.

SCALIA: That is not access, no.

ASHMORE: If I can establish the fact that my point of view is not represented in your treatment of a public issue, and you are ordered to meet my demand, isn't that access?

SCALIA: It is the Fairness Doctrine you have just described, and all that requires is that on major controversial issues of public importance diverse views must be presented. It doesn't require that any particular individual be allowed to present those views, and that is an important distinction for Mr. Salant and Mr. Frank, who are professional journalists, and who insist on their right to find the best people to present views and determine the way in which such views ought to be presented. That right remains intact. No individual can come into a station and demand the right to make a speech.

ASHMORE: Even if I can't go on the air in person, if I can go to court and demonstrate that my view has not been heard and I can get a court order that requires you to open up, isn't that an important form of access?

THOMAS H. WOLF: What the people who cry access really want is to have their position more persuasively presented to a bigger audience. You might even deny access in this sense by opening up a kind of electronic Hyde Park, which would guarantee everybody the right to say his piece without regard to the audience factor—what I expect would happen if cable systems are required to set aside a channel for use by anybody who has something to say on a public issue. In Brazil at the moment the government has commandeered the hour between six and seven at night on all radio and television stations to present its own views. That period is known popularly as the hour of silence. Nobody looks or listens.

LLOYD CUTLER: Mr. Carlson, I take it, in essence is suggesting that we might substitute some general right of public access for the present Fairness Doctrine. I wonder if the public would really like that.

CARLSON: There seems to be a great reluctance to trust the public on matters of news, but a great deal of trust in the public when it comes to matters of commerce.

SALANT: If we're really talking about broadcasting and the First Amendment, what we have to decide is whether access is a good or a bad thing, constitutionally or extraconstitutionally, for print as well as broadcasting. Is there something special about broadcasting that subjects it to a constitutional principle that doesn't apply to print?

RONALD M. SEGAL: I confess with regret, and of course respect, that I do not understand what Mr. Salant is talking about, and less so since I took the trouble to read two documents which issue from his pen, both of them full of Miltonic sentiments and invocations of liberty. The issue of access seems to me not entirely irrelevant in those terms.

Whose interests are we discussing? Is it the interest of the newscasters, is it the interest of the stockholders of the Radio Corporation of America, is it that of the Republican Party, or is it that of a decent democracy with which one would assume the First Amendment has something to do? The question of who should be licensed, and whether there should be licensing at all, follows from this.

PORTER: What evils and abuses do you have in mind that should be remedied, and how?

SEGAL: I think it is, on the surface, absurd to say that we live in a free society when mass communications are owned by a few people. I think it is self-evident that TV operates as an industry for its own purposes, I would say those of profit. To say that all citizens in this or any other social democratic state have free access to mass communications is nonsense. It is the general policies of the proprietorship, transmuted through professional producers and newscasters, that largely determine not only who appears on these networks but what issues are discussed. The society seethes with dissenting views that create major issues only when people take to the streets. The Vietnam war came to notice first in the streets of America, and only then became an issue. Does anyone here seriously suggest that a privately owned company does or could exist with its major object the free flow of information from gatherer to consumer?

PORTER: Doesn't that lead you logically to government ownership and operation?

SEGAL: No. To give such powers to the state is to go the way of peoples' democracies in Eastern Europe. You just substitute for the vested interests of the proprietor the vested interests of the communications bureaucracy or some other manifestation of the government.

PORTER: Somebody has to decide something.

SEVAREID: As a matter of fact, some of the most controversial minority complaints became major issues only because television recognized their importance and gave them a boost. Take the matter of cigarettes and cancer, which certainly went against the corporate grain of networks which used to derive major revenue from tobacco accounts. Ed Murrow made that an issue. As to Vietnam, there were raging quarrels on radio and television about the validity of the intervention in Southeast Asia long before there were any demonstrations in the streets. For many years the burden of the criticism of the mass media followed Mr. Segal's line. It came from left-liberal intellectuals who said television merely reflected the middle-class status quo, and deified bourgeois values. Agnew came along and said the exact opposite, and tapped a big reservoir of resentment on the part of those who said the networks were coddling the minorities, paying too much attention to militant blacks and militant students, and exalting violence as a means of social change.

WOLF: Mr. Segal seems to assume that because the networks and the individual broadcasters are profit-making organizations it follows that their news operations are constrained to conduct themselves so as to be certain to make money. I can assure you that everybody that I have ever known or met in television would deny that.

SEVAREID: Including the newsmen on the firing line.

ROGERS: To reinforce the views of my colleagues, Mr. Sevareid and Mr. Wolf, it ought to be pointed out that this country was able to create almost overnight a miraculous mass communications system precisely because it is a product of the marketplace. If the mass media were instead a platform for the dissident elements in the society, it could not serve a mass audience because the majority wouldn't be tuned in.

ASHMORE: Coming back to the First Amendment, I'd like to ask Mr. Salant if his principal concern is not that the Nixon administration's version of access will require him to abandon some degree of the control he now has over selection and presentation of the news, and that he is invoking the First Amendment principally against that threat.

SALANT: What concerns me is not the Nixon administration. We have learned by now that each administration improves on its predecessor in its ability to try to get at us through our bosses or through our affiliates or through the courts or through the FCC. I think we make a great mistake in personalizing this. I would guess that we have much less to fear from the Nixon administration on the question of access than we have from a successor administration—if, for example, Nick Johnson became president. I do not see this as a partisan issue.

ASHMORE: In that regard, do you agree that there is a fairly broadly based public demand for access which takes the form of protest against what you are now doing, that substantial segments of the public—on the left, on the right, and in the middle—consider the performance of the media inadequate in their own terms?

SALANT: Yes, but I don't think you can deal with that in terms of access. There is a great uneasiness among what I call the sub-publics—all of the sub-publics—because they're not seeing and hearing what they want to see and hear. They are not asking to get on the air on their own behalf; they're demanding that CBS find a Sevareid who will comment on the news so that they can nod their heads up and down instead of from side to side. I don't think it is our function to meet that demand.

ASHMORE: Still, there is presumably something that can be called the public's right to know, and that embodies the expectation that the media will present all points of view. That involves something significantly different from the expectation of agreement—and many more or less reasonable viewers and readers doubt that the media are performing that function adequately.

SALANT: Certainly I am concerned about the lack of credibility, the disenchantment, the apparent general alienation of news consumers, if you want to call them that. I am only suggesting that the problem of credibility can be exaggerated for partisan purposes—and I suspect that some of those who bring it up are willing to throw out the baby along with the bath water.

CARLSON: One reason the First Amendment issue comes up in relation to the question of credibility is that the great majority of information that reaches us comes through very few filters. That is simply a fact. Now, the First Amendment says the Congress shall make no law to constrain the private operators of these filters. I suggest we ought to try to define what these evolving concepts mean in light of current technology, and the forms of concentration it has produced.

SALANT: Are they different for broadcasting than they are for print?

CARLSON: I think they are, but I haven't gone into it. . . .

SALANT: I suspect that they are too, but let's try to define the difference—try to spell out why the right of access should be different, larger, smaller, or whatever, for broadcast than it is for print. That's what we're really talking about.

ROGERS: The fact of the matter is that all of our dancing around the question of whether the Fairness Doctrine is consonant with the First Amendment is academic. What a local station owner is concerned with is the license-renewal process. At that point, what is germaine is the ream of FCC instructions that have the force of law on the licensee at renewal time. They instruct him that he will engage in a procedure now called ascertainment. Ascertainment means to a station manager that he will, by God, see to it that people seeking access get access. This creates a fear complex, and it speaks to issues that so far we have not faced in this discussion.

Whether the First Amendment actually requires that people in general have access to somebody's cameras or microphones or printing press is academic as far as I am concerned, because I know that the Federal Communications Commission, under its accretion of power and the building of administrative law on top of administrative law, requires me to provide what they call ascertainment of community needs. This means that the station manager is no longer the chief salesman, he is the chief fellow who goes around the community for three years trying to find out if anybody has a bitch and, if so, to make sure he finds a way to get him on the air so he will not be able to claim to the FCC that he was denied access. As one who has gone through this routine, I can tell you that it is a chamber of horrors alongside what Whitehead suggested.

KALVEN: Isn't that mostly paper work—it's a nuisance if you have to do it, but does it really turn out that the ascertainment process has any teeth in it?

ROGERS: Let me give you one concrete example of what kind of teeth it has in it. One of the stations in my company had its license challenged, along with all of its competitors in a particular community, by a group that called itself a black coalition. The challenge was predicated upon the charge that the station had violated the rights of the black minority by not having adequate minority hiring and training practices, and that it had not given sufficient weight to minority tastes in entertainment and cultural affairs and so forth. The fact of the matter was that at the time the petition was brought the station had more than a numerical quota of blacks in terms of community percentage. That demonstrable and readily measurable fact did not relieve us of battling for renewal—which I remind you means survival—against a group so unrepresentative of the community they professed to speak for that by the time the administrative procedure came to an end every single one of them was either in jail for felony or had moved out of town. We got our renewal, but not before the process had resulted in a legal bill and attendant costs on the order of a quarter of a million dollars. This is not an isolated example. It is happening time after time after time after time after time.

CHAPTER 5

# THE PUBLIC
# NETWORK

---

I N THE EARLY 1920s, Herbert Hoover, as Secretary of
Commerce under President Harding, had thrust upon
him the unhappy task of dealing with a cacophony of unlicensed and uncooperative broadcasters jamming the airwaves with their roving radio signals. Mr. Hoover seems to
have been shocked by the notion that, once the government
had sorted out the mess, a great new advertising enterprise
might spring into being. The Great Engineer thought of radio as a means of personal communication, with some application as a conveyor of culture and education to the masses,
and at the Washington Radio Conference in 1922 he said, "It
is inconceivable that we should allow so great an opportunity
for public service to be drowned in advertising chatter."

Although it prevailed in Great Britain and Canada, and in
most European countries, the idea of broadcasting as a
public service, publicly financed, had effectively disappeared
in this country by the time the Federal Radio Commission
was established by President Coolidge in 1927. When FRC
became FCC in 1934, CBS was a going concern, and NBC
had two radio networks, one of which would be spun off to

become ABC. Advertisers were standing in line to provide funds for the creation of a major new home entertainment medium upon which an embryonic audio-journalism rode piggyback.

In the case of radio and its successor, television, the FCC did reserve some channels for what was termed educational broadcasting, issuing special licenses requiring that these stations be publicly owned and non-commercial. Many of these slots in the broadcast band were never filled, and the stations that did emerge in the major cities found that, while they were specifically denied income from advertising, they could command only a thin trickle of funds from the only sources left to them—philanthropy, volunteer contributions, and educational institutions that considered themselves already impoverished. These non-commercial stations struggled along in comparative obscurity until 1967, when the Corporation for Public Broadcasting was created with a commitment for federal funding.

What came to be called the "fourth network" was recommended by a high-level commission set up and financed by the Carnegie Corporation with the blessing of President Lyndon B. Johnson. The proposal was for a nonprofit government corporation with the mission of expanding and greatly improving "educational TV." At the beginning of 1973 there were 224 of these public broadcasting stations operated by community boards, school systems, universities, and state and municipal agencies. Most of these came into being over the fifteen-year period in which the Ford Foundation put up $225 million to finance station construction, experimental programming, and related services. Under a special grant-in-aid act, the federal government contributed another $67 million for improving and expanding physical broadcast facilities.

By the time the Carnegie Corporation made its report, it was clear that the needs of educational TV had far outstripped the income it could expect from these sources. If the stations were to be pulled together to produce programming of a technical and artistic quality comparable to that provided by commercial TV, the new national system would require a major source of guaranteed annual income. There was no possible "sponsor" except the federal government.

Some idea of the gap that had to be covered may be seen in the fact that the 195 public stations on the air in 1970 represented 28.2 percent of the 690 commercial stations but enjoyed only 6.2 percent of the total station revenue. The commercial stations were grossing over a *billion* and a half dollars, and spending over a *billion* and a quarter on station operations, while the ETV outlets were spending only 107 *million* and going in the hole at that.

The Carnegie Corporation estimated that it would require $338 million in annual operating costs, and a capital outlay for new stations and equipment of $621 million, to bring into being a complete national service embracing the 380 stations necessary for country-wide coverage. In 1972 a study by the Aspen Program on Communications and Society estimated minimum annual operating cost to maintain quality standards at $431,844,000.

Federal funds for operating purposes began to be channeled through CPB in 1967, and the new corporation used them to finance a cable interconnection that made possible the first truly national programming available to the starveling educational stations. By thus greatly increasing the potential audience for a given program beyond the capacity of any individual outlet, the interconnection justified expenditures for dramatic, cultural, and public affairs programming on a scale comparable to that of the commercial networks. By 1971 the CPB stations were receiving an average of 36.5 percent of their programming through national, regional, or other interconnection, against 23 percent of programming locally originated. The result of this infusion of quality has been a signal increase in audiences, with some metropolitan PBS stations at their peak hours for the first time providing the commercial broadcasters real competition for public attention.

In its October, 1972, report on the financial requirements of public broadcasting, the Aspen Program on Communications and Society concluded:

> The nation can well afford a quality nationwide public television service. Although it is impossible to assign a dollar figure to the benefits from such a service, the levels of support for public broadcasting in other countries provide an indication of the value placed on such services outside the United States. Federal government support for public television amounts (on a per capita basis) to $5.81 in Canada, to $3.29 in the United Kingdom, and to $2.90 in Japan. In contrast, total public television system support in the United States amounts to 80¢ per capita, only 17¢ of which was provided by the 1971–72 CPB appropriation. Our estimates indicate that an increase of $1.27 per capita for annual operations is required.

The Aspen study affirms the earlier finding of the Carnegie Corporation that the only possible source of the necessary funds is federal financing. And, although the contribution of the federal government is still only a niggardly fraction of total expenditures, that necessity has plunged the new-found CPB into the very center of the controversy between the Nixon administration and the media.

The Carnegie Corporation recommended that CPB receive long-range financing, preferably from an earmarked license or other levy, to insulate its operations from the political pressures inherent in annual congressional appropriations. But that feature went by the board in the horse trading that attended CPB's birth under the nominal supervision of fifteen directors appointed by the President and confirmed by the Senate. John Macy, CPB's first president and most conspicuous martyr, recalls the whispered advice of wise old Washington hands to avoid all controversy, play it safe, stick to symphony concerts and children's programs—at least until the annual appropriation became a habit and CPB had acquired a testy old champion among the congressional elders.

However, as Macy understood it, CPB's mandate was to construct "one or more systems of interconnection" to permit live, instantaneous broadcasts on topical subjects. The Carnegie Commission had foreseen a major role for CPB in experimenting with new forms and techniques of video journalism as a contrast and possible goad to the commercial broadcasters, who were lapsing into stereotypes in their entertainment format and in their handling of news and public affairs. E. B. White defined the mission as a need "to restate and clarify the social dilemma and political pickle." Macy and his board concluded that public broadcasting would fail in its primary mission if it turned its cameras away from the stormy landscape of public controversy.

Macy did not participate in the conference on Broadcasting and the First Amendment, but in a later visit to the Center he gave his version of the events leading up to the crippling administration attack on CPB:

In establishing a system linking more than 200 "educational" stations for program distribution, we recognized the essential involvement of the local licensees in program selection and scheduling, and in the coordination of the expanding circle of production sources CPB was bringing into being. To that end, the Public Broadcasting Service (PBS) was formed in 1970 as the instrument through which the stations would work in close collaboration with CPB, but at one remove from the federal funding source. We accepted for CPB the role of providing a heat shield protecting the system from the political fire that might be generated by controversial public affairs or cultural programming.

To provide a professional journalistic base in Washington, the National Public Affairs Center for Television (NPACT) was formed by the leadership of the local station (WETA), augmented by a national board drawing directors from business, labor, journalism, law, and education. The NPACT charter assumed responsibility for Washington-originated or related projects for national distribution.

There was no regular news programming as such, but there was provision for coverage of congressional hearings, presidential speeches, and for expert reaction and analysis after such events. Also NPACT was to have a key role in interpreting the coming national election.

This was the area where sensitive nerves were struck. Certain individual programs, although limited in number in relation to the total inventory, created a storm of controversy. Liberal journalists perceived signs of CPB caving in to government pressure, conservative spokesmen claimed that CPB failed to exercise adequate control over programming, and more neutral critics questioned the quality and fairness of the journalistic effort. The ability of a government-financed broadcast system to exercise press freedom clearly was at issue.

The strain proved intolerable for the delicate structure of collaborative decision-making which gave all parties an active voice in programming. Editorial judgments, interpretations of issues, and choice of personnel sparked intramural rivalries among the several special interests within the system, and rendered all parties more vulnerable to outside pressures.

At this point the benign neutrality with which the Nixon Administration seemed to look upon Public Broadcasting vanished. In October, 1971, a dissenting judgment on the entire CPB development was delivered by Clay T. Whitehead, director of the White House Office of Telecommunications Policy, before the public broadcasters assembled at Miami Beach.

His attack was intensely political, and in line with charges the Administration was beginning to bring against the commercial media. The broadside was obviously designed to shake the uneasy public broadcasting structure by condemning the alleged centralization of CPB and PBS, while courting the stations through financial recognition for the "bedrock of localism." Whitehead followed up in a radio interview:

"There is a real question as to whether public television, particularly the national federally funded part of public television, should be carrying public affairs, news commentary, and that kind of thing . . ."

We had anticipated trouble with Congress, but objections from Capitol Hill were reasonable and infrequent until the Executive Branch began to orchestrate the attack. As a final irony, while publicly deploring centralized authority in CPB and PBS, Administration representatives behind the scenes were applying pressure on the same organizations to exercise more control over offending journalists.

The campaign culminated in late 1972 with the President's veto of the CPB authorization bill, the addition of six Nixon-appointed board members, and the selection of Henry Loomis as president following my protest resignation. Congress had passed with bipartisan majorities a two-year extension providing increased funding for CPB. But the White House applied the *coup de grâce,* and the President's veto message was a delayed rerun of the indictment issued by Whitehead eight months earlier in Miami Beach.

The conclusion has to be that the heat shield has been penetrated, and video journalism, public style, severely burned. At this point, the endeavor to establish freedom of expression in non-commercial broadcasting must be deemed a failure.

The administration fuglemen who defend the ruthless reconstitution of CPB concede most of the facts as set forth here, but charge that Macy and his colleagues were proceeding under an erroneous interpretation of the enabling act, and had evolved an indefensible theory and practice for publicly financed broadcasting. The White House version of the legislative history of CPB rejects the idea that a primary justification for public broadcasting is the need to fill the minority audience void, and thereby provide a non-commercial yardstick to measure the performance of broadcasters who are dependent upon advertising, and subject to pressure toward bland, common denominator programming. The counter-view is that if there is to be public financing there is bound to be political pressure—and the only way to meet this threat is to emasculate public broadcasting so as to remove any possible excuse for its being brought to bear.

At the Center conference Antonin Scalia developed this argument in exchanges with James Loper, head of the public broadcasting station and key program facility in Los Angeles, and immediate past chairman of PBS.

SCALIA: I didn't mean to be facetious when I suggested that we have not been talking about what the First Amendment requires, but about whether we really want the First Amendment. I think the difference in treatment of the media is attributable to an accidental social judgment made a long time ago. What has happened with the advance of the electronic media is that we have simply lost our innocence. We have tasted the forbidden fruit of censorship, and I am afraid we don't find it so bad.

Our discussions here demonstrate this. Everybody at one stage decries government involvement, the specter of government control, and then you hear the same people decrying the lack of balance, the fact that certain people can't disseminate their views. Well, you can't have it both ways. You are either going to let the media perform as they will, no matter how badly they serve the public, or else you are going to try, through government, to impose some standards of responsible performance. Either way may be feasible— both have been tried by other governments.

The American way, under the First Amendment, conceived in the days when we only had local printed media, held that we had to keep government out of communications, and leave it to the people to see that somehow truth would prevail. Through a series of accidents—I am sure nothing really can be said to be premeditated under the working of the Federal Communications Act—we have gone down the road toward the other way of doing things. And, I am sorry to say, I don't see that everybody finds the results bad.

As a glaring example, I find here people who profess to be deeply concerned over the problems of government control of the media but who also ardently support a scheme to establish a national television network, with a centralized system of news and public affairs programming that is dependent upon the government for its operating income.

The fact that we can talk about more independence for the press on the one hand, and on the other hand say, but what we really need is a government-funded national news operation, strikes me as wild. It is just wild. I cite this as evidence of the essential schizophrenia that underlies every discussion I have ever heard about the First Amendment and the press. We love it and we hate it.

KALVEN: I have to agree with Mr. Scalia that these discussions are—I wouldn't say schizophrenic, but I would say ambivalent. This turns up on at least two fronts. One is the ambivalence between First Amendment applications to the print and the broadcast media, where we find ourselves having different reactions, depending on whether the news is to be read or heard and seen. The other ambivalence derives from the economic arena in which the media have their being. The tradition of the law is that there is something like a preferred position for the press. Now, if you move toward absolutes to resolve the ambivalence, you'll be paying a price in one direction or the other. No one can claim that the First Amendment isn't a calculated gamble. The defense is that we have found it a prudent and elegant gamble.

ASHMORE: I will only volunteer for myself, but I am willing to dispose of one ambivalence that has plagued us. I will concede that the problem of access, the contention that the right to speak freely doesn't mean anything unless you have the means to reach the mass audience, probably has become just as acute in the case of the print media as it is in broadcasting. In other words, my First Amendment right to set up my own press without government interference doesn't mean much if I have to use a mimeograph machine to try to create a countervailing force to the *Los Angeles Times*.

But I do not concede Mr. Scalia's charge of schizophrenia against those who oppose government interference with the media and also support government financial support for non-commercial public affairs broadcasting. I do not concede that the central government has any more right to dismantle a public network than it does a private one if the reason is that those who happen to be in office dislike its public affairs programming. As I understand what has happened to the Corporation for Public Broadcasting and the Public Broadcasting Service, this is what is being done—although, of course, the excuse is that all this is merely a return to localism.

SCALIA: The administration position on public broadcasting —and I was counsel to the Office of Telecommunications Policy when this happened, so I can speak authoritatively as of that time—was always very much in favor of localism, which is the spirit that the Public Broadcasting Act of 1967 breathes. The administration legislative proposal for 1972

would have given a substantial amount of the public broadcasting funds to the local stations as a matter of right. CPB
opposed that formula because it wanted to be able to say
who could get money and who couldn't get money. So the
administration bill, which certainly was very much in favor
of localism, did not pass because of CPB opposition. Instead,
Congress passed a bill that increased the money and gave
CPB full control over how to spend it. The President vetoed
that bill. There has been no inconsistency whatever in the
administration position on public broadcasting. It is in favor
of localism.

SEVAREID: But here is the administration saying that there
are too few national sources of news and documentaries and
opinion, and at the same time knocking down the fourth network which the non-commercial stations operated as Public
Broadcasting Service.

SCALIA: The administration had nothing to do with eliminating PBS, just as it had nothing to do with creating it. PBS
was created, and is being curtailed, by the Corporation for
Public Broadcasting, which is not the administration.

SEVAREID: Oh, look, John Macy was thrown out, and the
President's own man, Henry Loomis, was put in there for
the purpose of dismantling certain programming.

PORTER: He must have had pretty good backing when he
could knock off Bill Buckley and Sander Vanocur at one
stroke.

LOPER: I must say, Tony, that I have had a number of discussions with you and with Clay Whitehead over the years

I served as chairman of PBS, and I simply can't resolve the basic anomaly of your position. A year ago in October we were told that public broadcasting was to rest on the bedrock of localism, and ever since every indication has been that the administration—and I will not buy the argument that the reorganized CPB and the administration are not synonymous—is moving toward a concentration and centralization of all of the decision-making now dispersed through the whole system. Certainly, the decision-making is being taken away from the stations themselves, as they were represented by PBS. I have been sitting right in the middle of this reorganization, and this is what I have seen happening over the last eighteen months.

SCALIA: Jim, I have two points. Point number one—and this is also in response to Eric—the decision on concentration taken by CPB was not the administration's decision. I have been out of the area for a couple of months now, as you know, and I personally don't think I like it; I personally would have preferred to go the other way. But the fact is that the beginning of the centralization of authority in CPB occurred, as you know, under John Macy when there was a flap during the summer over a couple of programs. The result was that CPB established tighter controls over the kind of programming PBS was putting out, and then PBS also established a sort of oversight board, so I don't think you can say centralization is a result of administration action in any sense. I think it is a result of CPB's recognition of the inevitable difficulty of public broadcasting—that CPB would get the blame when there is programming that the public at large does not like. Voters write to their congressmen to protest, whereupon the congressmen don't allocate the kind of money the public broadcasters would like.

You could hardly have expected that situation to continue indefinitely, unless the appropriation bill gives the money directly to the stations, which is what we proposed. If you are going to have CPB in charge, then CPB is going to take the responsibility. I think that is inevitable.

ASHMORE: But the fact is that Congress increased the appropriation for CPB, and the President vetoed it.

MINOW: Well, the practical result, and I speak as the chairman of the public television station in Chicago, is that we no longer have any resources to do any programming. The veto, and the reorganization of CPB and PBS, has left us without the means to perform our service to the public. Even though we break our back to raise local funds, we can't do the kind of job we ought to be doing.

SCALIA: The station should have supported the administration bill. Now, I can understand Jim Loper's feelings, but he is just dead wrong when he talks about the destruction of the fourth network. There should never have been a fourth network. The Public Broadcasting Act of 1967—and this is something that most of you in this room probably don't realize—specifically stated that the Corporation for Public Broadcasting was not to own or operate any system of interconnection. It was specifically intended by the Congress that it was not to form a network. Now, to my mind, CPB evaded that proscription by setting up a wholly controlled creature, PBS, which in turn owned and operated a network.

LOPER: But, Tony, CPB is specifically charged with setting up systems of interconnection. Now, whether you call that a network or a system, it comes out the same way.

SCALIA: No, it could set up a system or systems without having the whole thing in control of one centralized network.

ASHMORE: Since we can't seem to agree on what is happening to public broadcasting in this country, maybe we ought to take a look at a publicly financed system that has been in operation for many years. . . .

LORD RITCHIE-CALDER: On the question of government-financed broadcasting, the British experience is in point. I find the analogies very close; we, too, started off nervously with radio, originally simply allocating wave lengths. The job was assigned to the Post Office, and since the Postmaster General is responsible to Parliament, the question of political control of broadcasting came up at once. Our solution was the British Broadcasting Company, with a charter that vested in its director-general the responsibility for seeing that the worst affronts to human dignity—obscenity and all that sort of thing—never sullied the airwaves. In carrying out that charge we have had some extreme forms of censorship, but very little trouble on the purely political side.

The BBC derives its income from license fees charged annually against radio and television sets, and so it is independent of annual appropriations by Parliament. BBC operates its own programming and broadcasting facilities. There is also an Independent Television Authority, which supervises the program companies that serve the commercial broadcasting stations deriving revenue from advertising. This authority also is a public body under even more strict restraints than BBC. The ITA doesn't own or administer the local commercial stations, but it does lay down directives for programming, and, like the FCC, it can issue and revoke licenses. Both BBC and ITA maintain advisory councils on a regional basis to provide a cross section of public reaction and response. All these feed back through the board of governors to the director-general of BBC, and in the case of the ITA, to the staff.

Now, I spent much of my life as a practicing journalist, and I cannot conceive, and nobody around this table, I hope, can conceive of any way such interlocking committees and advisory boards can actually control what is going to be put on the air. It's impossible. All that can be done is to lay down certain principles. This is what these public agencies do in Britain, and if there is a kickback, that is reflected in their next set of strictures.

You may recall the recent flap over the BBC's program "Yesterday's Men," which the Labour Party leaders protested was a travesty of Harold Wilson and others. The BBC fought back and justified its right to put on the program. But after it was all over, BBC agreed that perhaps this was not the proper way to do things—although, of course, this concession had nothing to do with whether Harold Wilson didn't like what BBC did to him. Thus there is restraint in the feedback from outside, the public reaction. Also the broadcasters and the press work under strict statutes—the Libel Act, the Obscenities Act, the Official Secrets Act—which are much more stringent than American laws. And every judge, on his own motion, has the right to censor through prior restraint. That has happened recently to both the *London Times* and BBC.

ASHMORE: Could I ask you to make a highly subjective judgment? You have spent a lot of time in this country, you have been here consistently now for the last six months. Would you think public confidence in the broadcast and print media in Britain is higher than it is in the United States?

RITCHIE-CALDER: In Britain it is higher. BBC always has been very, very scrupulous—although sometimes unimaginative and unenterprising. The ITA news is provided by program companies which are wholly autonomous and generally free of any suspicion of influence by advertisers or commercial interests.

ASHMORE: You think the British public's confidence in the journalistic function of the media is fairly high?

RITCHIE-CALDER: I should say it's fairly high. Some of us are critical of the entertainment side, where you get all the questions of taste and values, the unmeasurables. But I would say that if I compared the news I get on TV and radio with that I get from the eleven newspapers I read in Britain, it stands up solidly.

ASHMORE: Would you say that the communications system, if you are taking it on the whole in Britain, is any less or any more establishmentarian than ours?

RITCHIE-CALDER: Oh, well—there is one thing in this wicked world we've got to live with—our best news services are elitist. They must be. But the curious thing is that BBC has always been accused of being left-wing. God knows it isn't, really, but it has always been accused of being left-wing, I think, because younger people are on the job there, who've got imagination, and—

PORTER: But your commercial media are virtually undistinguishable from ours, aren't they?

RITCHIE-CALDER: That's right. I would say that all the considerations that might influence a commercial system influence the ITA—and since BBC is competing for audience, it is not immune to the popularity contest aspect. Our newspapers, of course, are all dependent upon advertising.

The mirror-image quality of the Nixon administration's treatment of public broadcasting is illustrated in one of the few personal comments the President has placed on the record. He wants to see the non-commercial system structured, he has said, so that "it would be impossible or at least extremely difficult for either this administration or any succeeding administration to make a propaganda arm out of it."

If one were to take that mandate literally, the White House complaints of CPB bias would seem to be the best evidence that this worthy goal has been achieved. The charges against the public broadcasters are, in any case, overblown and in many cases palpably ridiculous. The ideological range of viewpoints excised from public network programming under the ministration of the Nixon appointees is from William Buckley on the right to the moderate, homespun Bill Moyers on the left. In between were such essentially analytical efforts as Washington Week in Review, which featured a panel of the top Washington newspaper and magazine correspondents, and the thoughtful, low-key political profiles by Elizabeth Drew.

As to NPACT's coverage of the presidential campaign, this was essentially a worthy if not always successful effort to take TV beyond the commercial networks' redundant concentration on familiar political figures. It was the public network's ambition to use its cameras to trace the nomination and election process as it began at the precinct level—the grass roots, that is, to which homage is now being paid by NPACT's executioners. Flawed as it was, this was probably the most sustained effort at journalistic localism ever undertaken by national TV. It follows that the administration's case against NPACT never produced chapter and verse to sustain the charge of bias, but was primarily centered on the $85,000 salary CPB offered its senior political correspondent, Sander Vanocur, to hire him away from NBC. Although this was a marketplace determination, in which Vanocur actually took a cut in income, it was bound to be a key issue in the infighting, since it established a level of pay higher than that of a congressman or a White House aide.

The scuttling of these programs required the subordination of the PBS, since, on the basis of more than a year's experience, the major public stations valued them as essential contributions to their total broadcasting pattern and had audience ratings to sustain their judgment. Despite this showing from the grass roots, there were indications that the new masters of CPB would not approve their transmission on the fourth network interconnection if money were no object—even if, as had been indicated, the Ford Foundation and other private sources agreed to provide the funds to finance production.

In the face of this controversy, Thomas B. Curtis, the President's hand-picked chairman of CPB, continued to claim his board's support in principle for public affairs broadcasting, and offered this pledge of his own faith: "There are people in the White House who feel that you can't do public affairs objectively and with balance, and therefore, they would throw the baby out with the bath water. And there are people in Congress who also say that. I happen to think one can argue a point of view and do it with objectivity and balance."

Even if one could imagine that the Curtis standard would permit programming more forthright than the arithmetically balanced *Advocates*, it appears that the chairman's view became moot almost as soon as he had uttered it. Curtis and

Loomis appeared before the Senate Communications Sub-committee late in March, 1973, to strongly urge that CPB be funded for two years at an increased rate of $60 million for 1974 and $80 million for 1975—in effect, the budget President Nixon vetoed after it had been offered by John Macy and approved by both houses. The CPB officials pointed out that the gestation period for high quality TV programming is many months, and that year-to-year budgeting presents an almost insurmountable handicap to coherent planning.

Immediately behind Curtis and Loomis came Clay T. Whitehead with a refutation on behalf of President Nixon. Long-range funding for public broadcasting is not acceptable to the President at this time, Whitehead told the subcommittee. The White House emissary accused the reconstituted CPB and the beleaguered PBS of trying to maintain a fourth TV network, and said that Mr. Nixon firmly opposes any such operation and would not support multi-year funding until the existing system had been broken down. Whitehead told the subcommittee: "Decentralization of programming activities is the cornerstone of the public broadcasting structure. Local stations should play a major role in decision-making in matters of programming and ultimately must have a realistic choice available in deciding whether to broadcast any CPB-supported or distributed programs." He then proceeded to limit that choice by declaring that "reliance on federal monies to support public affairs programming is inappropriate and potentially dangerous."

The chairman of the subcommittee, Democratic Senator John Pastore of Rhode Island, responded bluntly: "You know, Mr. Whitehead, I have a very firm conviction that even though you dress up your statement with sweet words, you have an animosity toward this corporation and toward public broadcasting. You praise in one breath; and then by the next breath, you suffocate it."

Even sharper comment came from Republican Marlow Cook of Kentucky, who had demonstrated his loyalty to the White House by service as master of ceremonies at the Nixon inauguration: "You are very clear that you don't want a fourth network. . . . I happen to believe, as a father who has got five children, that I am damned sick and tired of what my children are watching on television. Educational television is giving them an opportunity for once to use the media the way it ought to be used. . . . I have got to tell you I don't believe you are doing your job for the boss. I have to tell you that."

The evidence continued to pile up, however, that Whitehead had the full backing of "the boss" on every real point at issue. Curtis engaged in a protracted effort to work out a compromise that would guarantee the local station organization a muted but effective policy voice in CPB decisions. Agreement was reached between a CPB negotiating committee and a group representing the stations, and announced without details as certain to be approved. When the Nixon-dominated board convened, however, with thirteen out of fourteen members present and voting, the compromise was summarily rejected. A week later Thomas Curtis joined the growing list of responsible CPB officials who have resigned in outspoken or implied protest against the White House takeover. "When it became clear that the White House was not respecting the integrity of the board," Curtis said, "then I couldn't defend it. . . ."

All in all, the Nixon approach to public broadcasting has been a revealing exercise that points up the administration's dependence on public relations technique. The real objectives have never been candidly admitted; as they have inescapably emerged, they have been blurred when possible by ideological frosting. When the administration's arguments are demonstrated to be factually shaky, the response is a personalized attack aimed at hitting the adversary wherever he may be vulnerable politically, or in terms of his own self-interest. This is a strategic design which necessarily leaves in its wake a substantial number of cast-off victims who may reasonably consider themselves betrayed, but if these have been discredited in advance they can do little damage to a self-righteous crusade conducted in the vibrant style perfected by President Nixon's spiritual adviser, Billy Graham.

All the evidence indicates that the hard-line right-wing view has prevailed throughout the attack on public broadcasting. This approach is summarized in an article by M. Stanton Evans, editor of the *Indianapolis News* and chairman of the American Conservative Union, written for *Human Events* and appropriately reprinted in the *Washington Star-News* upon the occasion of Curtis' resignation from CPB. Evans begins by dismissing the controversy over public broadcasting as further evidence that "what is needed on both sides of this debate is a further step to the outright abolition of tax-funded television." He concludes, "There is really no reason to have such a system in the first place. The specialized audiences it is meant to serve can be catered to much more effectively by cable and pay TV . . . without the use of anybody's tax dollars. . . ."

That thesis provided the bedrock for a typically discursive speech by Whitehead before a conference on cable system development delivered in Los Angeles immediately following his abrasive confrontation with Senators Pastore and Cook. Whitehead referred to public television as a "contradiction in terms" to his, and presumably the administration's, view that the entire television system in the country should be privately owned. TV can be free to offer diversity, he said, "only if the government isn't involved." He noted finally that he foresaw a "diminished need" for public broadcasting as pay television comes into being as a part of the cable system. And, as is customary on these occasions, he sought support for the White House campaign by dangling bait before the cable operators, indicating that "current thinking" embodied in his agency's study of policy recommendations is wholly favorable to the cable industry—that is, that the cable systems should not be classified as common carriers, which presumably would relieve them of any public service obligation and of any federal, state, or local regulation.

Interpreting the Whitehead speech as an expression of the administration's conviction "that the only good public television is dead public television," Cecil Smith, the veteran TV editor of the *Los Angeles Times,* wrote:

"He indicated that with the growth of pay TV via cable, which he enthusiastically approves, there will be less need for public TV to serve what he called 'specialized interests.'

"I assume that includes kids who watch Sesame Street and in the future will be able to see it only if they have enough coin in their penny banks. Which, of course, is a complete violation of what Sesame Street and, for that matter, public television, is all about.

"To me what public TV is about is the entire spectrum of cultural activity that is necessarily unavailable on commercial television except in exceedingly small, rare doses."

Smith went on to cite distinguished programming produced or distributed by CPB, including the Civilization series with Kenneth Clark, considered by many the finest program ever produced for broadcast; a number of notable dramatic productions; the Misterogers program for children; Bill Buckley's Firing Line; and NPACT's examination of TV advertising. All of these programs, he noted, were held to be incapable of attracting a national audience of the size commercial broadcasters consider essential for the sale of advertising. This was true even of the spectacular *VD Blues*, aimed at alerting young people to the dangers of the spreading epidemic of venereal disease, which reached an audience estimated at three million, and produced 225,000 "hot-line" calls from viewers seeking more information on VD.

"These programs are what public TV is all about," Smith wrote, "and they are not what commercial TV is about, and they are not what pay TV or cable TV or any other commercial venture is about. Kill it, as it appears the administration wants, and you kill something immensely important to the health of this country. Call it civilization."

# CHAPTER 6

# THE POLITICAL
# ATMOSPHERE

---

T HE MASS MEDIA are at once creators and creatures of public opinion. By reporting it, they spread and enhance controversy, and inevitably themselves become parties to it. In an unsettled time of the sort we are currently passing through, they are fated to earn the opprobrium traditionally accorded the bearer of bad tidings. With their economic taproots bedded firmly in the marketplace, they are ineluctably a part of the establishment, and for a decade they have been on the front line of a largely rhetorical but widespread populist assault upon the status quo.

By any measure, including their own increasingly edgy and self-righteous defensiveness, the credibility of the media has been declining. In 1966 a Harris poll gave newspapers a confidence vote of 29 percent, television 25 percent, and advertising in general 21 percent. In 1972 the same poll showed the print media down to 18 percent, television to 17 percent, and advertising to 12 percent.

This situation was ready-made for a president who combines a deep personal grievance against the media with a driving ambition to radically restructure a government he believes to have gone wrong under forty years of moderate, mildly liberal rule. The great new engine of television enables the occupant of the White House to bypass his political adversaries and take his case directly to the people. This becomes virtually an insurmountable advantage if he can eliminate from these channels, or effectively discredit in advance, critical appraisal of his policies and forthright reporting of his practices.

The Watergate hearings documented the manner in which the White House began to implement just such a design well before the end of President Nixon's first term. From the usual effort to manage the news through flattery, cajolery, threat, and reward, the men around the President moved on to what his legal counsel, John Dean III, described in a staff memorandum as "the use of the available machinery of government to screw our enemies." In an effort to devalue Dean's damaging testimony, the White House attempted to characterize this as nothing more than political business as usual —but Washington correspondents could recall no instance in which presidential dealing with the media had ever descended to such a level and attained such a concert. In the past, the most outraged of chief executives had been restrained by the recognition that they were transacting public business, and therefore could properly be regarded as subject to public accountability. Mr. Nixon simply rejected this concept in important respects, and asserted a right of absolute executive privilege he would finally defend in court. This attitude came to permeate the White House, and when the media protested in the name of the people's right to know, the response was a wide-ranging counterattack aimed at every point where they were vulnerable. The extent of that vulnerability was charted from experience by the participants in the Center conference.

RITCHIE-CALDER: In my active days in journalism, I don't recall being particularly worried about the British equivalent of the First Amendment. The question of the free press never arose in formal fashion—but I think it existed in our blood corpuscles. We were dealing with it day to day, fighting it out with our own proprietors, our own editors, as well as those on the outside who were trying to silence us or use us. The question was how to somehow regularize the behavior which most responsible journalists regarded as necessary so that hired hands could hold out against being compelled to do things that were distasteful, unreasonable, and at the extreme obviously against the public interest.

PORTER: We all know that newspaper proprietors and broadcasters are human beings with special interests, and so are editors and reporters—and so, of course, are politicians. So what we are really dealing with is a multiple adversary procedure. For example, 95 percent of the newspaper owners were against Franklin Roosevelt, and probably 95 percent of the working press were for him. That kind of balance didn't matter a damn to FDR, even though he kept right on winning elections. When I was at FCC, he was constantly leaning on me to get the newspapers out of broadcasting. We finally came out with a report that in effect grandfathered in the existing newspaper-owned broadcast facilities, but provided that henceforth the concentration of mass media under one ownership would be one element to consider in granting a license. That meant that a newspaper applicant came to bat with at least one strike on him and maybe two, depending upon the size of the market and the character of the competing applicants.

But as I reflect on our discussions here, I am more than

ever convinced that the adversary relationship between the media and the government is an essential value in our set of democratic institutions. And what I am frankly disturbed about is the current environment in Washington—indeed throughout the country. This political atmosphere, subconsciously or directly, has created a nationwide attitude toward the media of cynicism, of distrust, of opportunism. As an example of where this leads us, applications have been filed against the TV stations owned by the *Washington Post* in Jacksonville and Miami by prominent friends and supporters of the present administration. Is that punitive in character? Or are the applicants just going after a political reward? Or both? What will the Commission do when this matter comes on for final resolution?

These applicants apparently are technically, financially, and legally qualified. And under the statute the FCC is supposed to use the same standards on renewal as are used in initial applications—including the provisions we wrote in because FDR was sore at the newspapers back in the thirties. Now, is the *Washington Post,* with valuable properties for which they paid some forty million dollars, I believe, going to be taken to the woodshed because another President is upset?

It is reasonable to suspect so since the White House's hostile attitude toward the *Post* is well-known, and regularly documented by Mr. Nixon's spokesmen. I suspect that is the reason those applicants are willing to go to the considerable legal and other expense entailed in filing. Certainly there is a widespread belief that political mechanisms can be used to gain preference in obtaining these valuable licenses. That belief alone is enough to undercut the adversary relationship between the media and the government.

ASHMORE: Isn't some such leverage inherent in the relationship between government and media? It lies not only in the power available to the government to act officially, but the power to intimidate without acting at all in a formal, legal sense. I am not sure that traditional First Amendment protection would cover the cases you cite in Jacksonville and Miami involving the *Washington Post*. If the broadcast licenses were not involved, there might be threatened action under some application of antitrust theory. I lived through a case in which a newspaper believed—with what I consider good reason—that it was subjected to the threat of extinction through a spurious, politically motivated Internal Revenue Service claim of income tax evasion.

SCALIA: Well, I must say I don't think Mr. Porter is offering a very well-documented case. There is more than one over-filing in Miami. It isn't as though these stations aren't being filed against by other persons. The fact that one of the applicants happens to have been a friend of the President's . . .

SALANT: Only somebody inside the government, and outside the broadcasting business, would say that. The important thing is not what is actually happening—we have no way of knowing what that is. The important thing is how our colleagues, who have licenses, perceive it. Now, if you recall, six weeks after Vice-President Agnew made the speech in which he took out after the *Washington Post*, a group of Nixon friends and ex-business associates filed in Miami for the *Post* station there. They only dropped out after the *Post* had to spend an awful lot of money getting ready, and agreed to reimburse the contestants for their costs—which, as Joe Alsop said, is like paying a wolf's dental bill after he bites you. Add to that the fact that six weeks after the election, another group has moved in Miami and Jacksonville. Nobody can be sure this is coincidence. It has spread shock waves through the industry, and people who hold licenses all around the country are saying, Gee, I'd better watch my step here—look what happens if you incur the disfavor of the government.

PORTER: By the way, Dick, what ever happened to CBS's instant analysis after presidential addresses?

SALANT: They still go on.

ROGERS: Yeah, but how many local stations carry them?

SALANT: They may not be carried wherever you are, but Eric was still right there at our microphone after the last speech.*

SEGAL: Well, my heart's in my throat, or, some of you might suppose, in my head. I'd like to reopen the battle I started earlier. My principal problem is that I am not sure how serious we want to be about the threat that we are discussing.

* In June 1973, CBS issued a policy statement announcing the "instant analysis" by its commentators would be dropped, but that when appropriate the network would make rebuttal time available to opposition spokesmen. Salant accepted the new dispensation philosophically when it came down from on high, and Sevareid supported it on the ground that there often wasn't time for adequate post-speech analysis—particularly since advance texts of President Nixon's addresses were becoming increasingly rare. There was, however, outspoken dissent in the ranks at CBS, and at the other networks, which did not immediately indicate whether they would follow suit. Robert Chandler, CBS vice president for public affairs, complained that the new policy confused fair comment with rebuttal: "This implies that in analyzing a speech we are necessarily taking an opposing view. That is not so. I think it's our responsibility, when a President comes off the air, to say what has been said and what the highlights of the speech were." It was noteworthy that CBS continued to join the other networks in providing "instant analysis" of even complicated points of law during intermissions in the Watergate testimony, which it carried live in rotation with NBC and ABC.

If the threat is a merely marginal one, to the media in the marketplace, then we seem to be engaged in some form of collective spiritual uplift. If we regard this as a radical threat, as I do, then I think we should ask why it exists. I reject the notion that we are concerned with some kind of dance between the mass media of the marketplace and the government.

I think the people are in this, that the authoritarian thrust, not only in the United States but throughout Western Europe—even in happy, neutral, prosperous Switzerland—comes about because there is a populist movement, to use Mr. Ashmore's phrase, of the right.

The government speaks as a dove in this country, in the name of the ordinary people. It gets away with sheer bloody murder. Every attack on the way the mass media in this country are run is mounted in the name of the American people, who are being deceived and deluded by an elitist liberal establishment. I think, therefore, that the elitist liberal establishment should ask itself, not simplistically, why this kind of accusation gets so much support.

It is my impression, and I say this very tentatively—and I am sure you will not agree—that the managers, the liberal managers of the mass media, do treat people fundamentally with disrespect. They serve them the kind of commodity they think they will like, and the market for this commodity has become resentful, angry, and looks for someone to put these people in their place. I was struck when Mr. Loper said he did not discern a large number of people crying for access to his educational station. The average person gives up, Mr. Loper said, because he doesn't think that he can make any impact on his environment, and so his audience is not pressing for access to the mass media. This is about the most terrifying commentary on the nature of American democracy that I can imagine. And it is no answer to say, Well, after all, Agnew is attacking us from one side and you left-wing radicals are attacking us from the other, so we must be doing something right. I am profoundly convinced that liberal democracy faces an assault from populist totalitarianism that we can only confront by taking democracy and mass communications to the people.

To be positive for the moment, I see nothing objectionable in the idea that the people should be allowed to manage mass communications for themselves. Built into the whole system of democracy is the assumption that twelve people, selected by lot from among their peers, can decide on so delicate a matter as the innocence or guilt of one of their number, can sentence the man to imprisonment for life. They have no special qualifications for such jury service. We assume that they are capable as people of making such profound decisions. Are they therefore not capable, as people, of running a television station, a radio station, or a newspaper? I am totally convinced that if we do not look to this alternative, we will have the state move in everywhere in mass communications.

FRED WARNER NEAL: It seems to me a number of critical points are coming together—Mr. Frank's question about the difference between the treatment of TV and the treatment of the press, Mr. Porter's question about the environment in Washington, and Mr. Scalia's question about whether or not we really believe in the First Amendment.

Now, I think it might be useful to consider those questions in light of the original philosophical basis for the First Amendment. The abuses of the press, of course, are legendary, and they were at an extreme in this country in 1776. Still, when the Constitution was written, it justified toleration for such abuses as a necessary guarantee of untrammeled freedom of expression—concluding quite specifically that this condition was preferable to any form of government regulation. This proposition has been upheld, more or less, throughout the history of the country; the courts so far have left the philosophical and moral underpinning largely intact.

Now, in this light, the issue we are discussing has a certain novelty. No one can doubt that TV journalism is now the most important force in our communications system—that is, that a considerable majority of the people form their opinions about public events primarily on the basis of impressions received through TV programs. I regard this development with absolute horror, myself, but I can't challenge the fact.

It's also true, I think, that because of the nature of TV, the possibilities of abuse are greater, and arise in different quarters. This brings us back to Mr. Scalia's basic question: Do we really accept the philosophical and moral justification of the First Amendment in the face of these profound changes in our system of communications? I don't think any of us can answer that without reference to the contemporary political atmosphere in Washington and across the country. No matter what kind of laws and constitutional provisions we have, they are always susceptible to being perverted—and, indeed, overthrown—unless our leaders and a controlling majority of the people believe in them and conduct themselves with the kind of self-restraint and civility a democratic society requires.

LOPER: There are other lessons to be drawn from that history, and these explain why I am amused at Mr. Segal's view of the way the United States works. We aren't a very orderly people, and so we have had to settle for representative democracy, since true, participational democracy could only result in anarchy. We had a reminder of our national character in the early days of broadcasting. The government did not impose licensing on the broadcasters, the broadcasters came to government and asked that they be regulated to alleviate the total disruption of service that resulted when too many radio stations began operating on the same frequencies. There had to be some arbitrary method of sorting out all this noise on the air.

That proposition still controls in broadcasting. It is not an internally democratic business, because it must deal hour by hour with the allocation of time and resources. Ultimately somebody has to make a decision. It's a linear process. A single responsible person must make or approve the final decision as to what goes on the air at a given time. I do not believe it is possible for a voluntary community structure to draw up and maintain a broadcast schedule. It simply will not work. This is what Ritchie-Calder meant when he said you can't escape the label of elitist in a business where, necessarily, a comparatively few people will do the talking, and even fewer will have to decide who they are.

That's the nature of the problem we always get back to: Who can be trusted to maintain the public interest when he decides what goes on the air and who is going to utter it? It can be simply stated, but obviously we have not been able to cope with it.

WOLF: The question of fairness is, always, whose fairness? And what it comes down to is whether a group representing the government can more fairly judge than a group with fewer political irons in the fire. I think it's demonstrable that a group with irons in the fire cannot judge as well as a group without. That's the key to guaranteeing fairness by licensing, as far as fairness goes.

PORTER: All I could think of during Mr. Segal's eloquent plea for true democracy was a cartoon *The New Yorker* ran just before the election. Two guys are standing in a bar, and one is saying to the other: "President Nixon is no dope. If this country wanted moral leadership, he'd give it moral leadership."

CUTLER: I am probably going to lose my membership card in the Federal Communications Bar Association, but in answer to the basic question I don't think we are going to do much better than the Fairness Doctrine. One of the things that worries me most about the Whitehead proposals is that they also contain a premise, or an implication, that the administration would like to do away with the Fairness Doctrine—which would please many broadcasters, of course. But imagine where we might be if we substituted some much more subjective requirement for license renewal, albeit every five years rather than three. I can work up a pretty good nightmare imagining questions that might be asked to test a station's performance. After all, as someone said, the present test isn't necessarily that you have to be fair, but that you have to balance any unfairness on one side with some unfairness on the other.

The critical question, the one that gives urgency to what used to be an interesting, abstract exercise for intellectuals, is what motivates the administration now that it has come to recognize that broadcasting has made possible the creation of a truly national means of transmitting information and opinion. The networks are powerful engines that sometimes get in the way of the government's own desires to convey information and opinion on its own terms.

At the root of all this, I think, is the present government's interest in destroying or curtailing the national information media. That's why the Public Broadcasting Service is being dismantled—it is a national service. That's why local stations are being encouraged to develop their own news programming at the expense of the national commercial networks. I suppose any government in power might entertain a similar ambition, and, like this one, it might claim it is acting in self-defense.

I don't for a moment think that this would happen, but consider the possibility that all three networks might agree to endorse the same candidate for president, and turn their news departments over to people committed to the use of this great power to insure the election of their candidate. That, obviously, is a prospect that would frighten everyone in this room—no less than the prospect that the government might take over the networks and use them in the same way for its own ends. Well, both potentials are there. Any network can and does reach a third of the nation in one stroke, with the result that Eric Sevareid will be recognized by infinitely more people on any airplane than will Scotty Reston of the *New York Times*. That is why it is critically important to appreciate and defend the great power of national media so that they can continue to deal independently with the expanding power of national government. We must maintain the tension that was referred to earlier, and not let the networks be converted into glorified Associated Presses that simply transmit material pretty much as it comes from official sources.

SEVAREID: It's not the power of the press in this country that's grown so greatly in the last generation, it's the power of government. That's why I sometimes wonder if the Nixon administration knows what it's doing, in the long run, in this attempt to enhance localism in communications. The immediate danger is not monopoly, or the scarcity of sources, or the restrictions that result from concentration. If we are talking about how democracy goes bad, we must recognize that there is usually a preliminary stage to an oppressive and centralized government, and that results from the fragmentation of society.

What is the cement of any community? Communications is bound to be a principal element. We have had an enormous fragmentation of points of view, with resulting conflicts of interest, in the last ten or twelve years. This approaches intellectual anarchy. The yawning gap between the intellectual community and the political community is a most serious manifestation. The kind of thing that used to hold diverse groups together—the big magazines of general interest, *Look* and *Life* and *Saturday Evening Post* and the rest— these are all gone. Instead we have a great growth of specialized publications that appeal to small, closed groups who talk to themselves.

We have had an enormous growth in radio stations, and now there are 800 TV stations—and let's not forget that most news and public affairs programs are of local origination. On top of this, cable TV is coming with the promise of many more channels for local programming. The result is that even the President of the United States can't command a national audience unless he commands all the outlets. On the rare occasions when he opens up for an hour interview on a single network—with Smith of ABC or Rather of CBS—he winds up with only 14 percent of the listening audience.

So if this or any administration wants to break up the networks, cut them off at the knees, in the same way Mr. Nixon is trying to undercut Congress, the way to do it is through localism. In the middle distance I can see us moving toward the condition of France before World War II, when

I lived there. It was a nation of critics. Government was conducted in the front pages of the papers, about 47 of them, published in Paris every day. Nothing could get done. It was a kind of political/intellectual anarchy. So I would say that the immediate danger to this country is not the possible restrictions of communications monopoly but the reverse— the degeneration of public affairs journalism into a kind of Tower of Babel.

SCALIA: I would really hate to think it's only CBS News that's holding us together. Let me try to reply to a couple of points that have just been made. First of all, Mr. Cutler, I cannot for the life of me imagine where you derive your description of the content of the Office of Telecommunications Policy proposals. Whitehead has said explicitly that the bill does not affect the Fairness Doctrine. There is only one proposal that OTP has ever made in that regard, and that was made when I was general counsel, and described by me in a speech before the Federal Communications Bar Association. We proposed moving in the direction of liberalizing its application, arguing that the Fairness Doctrine should not be applied on a case basis, as FCC has done in recent years, but rather should be applied—as all the other FCC restrictions are applied—at license renewal time. That points precisely in the opposite direction from what you suggest.

As for hostility to national news media, the administration in examining various ways to preserve freedom surely must consider the possibility of monopolization and manipulation of the media. If there is a threat on the one hand from government, surely there is also a threat on the other hand from centralization in private hands. The Federal Communications Act, not President Nixon, sought a particular solution to this problem, and that is to disperse responsibility to the local stations. That's not something President Nixon made up. It's in the Federal Communications Act, and it was also in the Public Broadcasting Act.

It also happens to be the basic premise of the administration's whole approach to communications. We do not want a BBC, or the kind of national network maintained by France and Italy and Germany. Now, maybe some of you want to change to that approach. I personally think it would be a mistake. That doesn't mean that I, or anyone now in the White House, think NBC and ABC and CBS are not useful and needed. But I fear centralization in private hands just as much as I fear centralization in government hands. I argue that to the extent we can hear many voices, and have many people responsible for the news, the better off we are. And the best way to achieve that goal, as I see it, is to disperse responsibility among a number of station owners.

CUTLER: I don't have any notes with me, but I believe that Mr. Whitehead has indicated in television interviews that he would ultimately like to see the Fairness Doctrine done away with in favor of different tests.

ASHMORE: I have the text of the famous Sigma Delta Chi speech before me. In regard to the Fairness Doctrine, Mr. Whitehead said: "Virtually everyone agrees that the enforcement of the Fairness Doctrine is a mess." After a reference to some improvement by FCC in what he calls "a chaotic scheme of Fairness Doctrine enforcement," he goes on to say: "But the Fairness Doctrine approach, for all its problems, was, is, and for the time being will remain a necessity, albeit an unfortunate one." I suppose, in fact, you could interpret that either way.

CUTLER: That is the nature of our problem. As to the Communications Act, there is certainly nothing there intended to discourage networking; on the contrary, it was designed to encourage the creation of national broadcasting systems. Nothing I have said suggests that monolithic networks should be sacrosanct, able to compel the acceptance of their news and other programs throughout the country. I see the broadcast network as a unique national medium the President and others can use to reach a national audience. I suggest that this valuable service has come under attack, in large part, because it is uniquely national and therefore uniquely powerful. A medium that reaches so many people at one time is one to be feared if you have something to conceal. You don't have to worry about a cacophony of local voices because they will cancel each other out.

SCALIA: I agree in part. Such a concentration of power is clearly to be feared.

CUTLER: I said myself that since a network clearly possesses power, it can't argue that its power must not be exercised responsibly. I think we all agree with that. But it must be allowed to exist as an independent force, which it cannot be if it is subject to being curbed by acts of government.

ASHMORE: I am impressed by the fashion in which, in principle at least, there seems to be convergence between Mr. Scalia's view of what ought to be done and Mr. Segal's. Now Mr. Scalia, I take it, wants to push control out to the localities, as far as possible, and Mr. Segal wants to take it somewhere beyond that, to the people themselves. I can agree with Mr. Segal that there is nothing objectionable in his theory, but I also have to agree with Mr. Loper that I can't imagine any way to implement it.

What we are up against now is a new system which, aside from where the power is located, is one of enormous complexity, with its own built-in scarcities. Only so much manpower is, or can be, engaged in the journalistic business of putting together a picture of the world on which men can act, in Walter Lippmann's perceptive description. That picture will be determined in large part by what has to be the centralized decision-making process required to deploy the manpower and winnow its product. The question is whether it is a responsible decision-making process.

One of the new problems we face now as a result of the technological imperatives that came with broadcasting is what is called information overload. I suspect that the worst of the confusions that exist in this country may result from the fact that we are getting far more alleged information than any of us can handle. The result is that we are politically numbed. Add to this another new fact—the creation of a vast apparatus of self-serving public relations bureaucrats, governmental and corporate, working within the communications system but beyond the control of the media managers. Our survival, perhaps our sanity, requires that some trustworthy agency arbitrarily screen out much of this flow of trivia, and clearly brand much that survives as of dubious character and doubtful source. I know of no way that this can be done without delegating to some human agency the responsibility for making such decisions. This is, in fact, the highest editorial function, and I suggest that it has never been more difficult, or more important.

NORTON GINSBURG: But that still leaves us with the problem

of guaranteeing points of entry into this system for the people—and I mean we, the people, not they, the people. The decision-making process, as you say, has a life-and-death importance to us as citizens of a democracy. That is why we are not going to succeed in getting away from the problem of access to information without taking into account the right to be heard.

Mr. Minow has usefully reminded us that we have to talk about scarcity in economists' terms. The scarcity element in communications is not too dissimilar to that of other scarce common resources. Not everyone has access, for example, to the mining of petroleum resources, and therefore society must have regulatory mechanisms for dealing with that kind of problem. So it seems to me that some kind of regulation of communications is essential.

HARVEY WHEELER: I agree. Despite the reassurance of our legal eagles that the new legislation as proposed by Mr. Whitehead will change nothing, I think Mr. Scalia has made it clear that the intent of the Nixon administration is to make a basic change by permitting the present informal, administratively regulated rules of access to become part of regular legislative matters in litigation before FCC. That's potentially an extremely important change, and I think it will very likely lead in a direction the networks will not like.

This is all a part of what I understand to be Mr. Nixon's "New Federalism," a manifestation of the ideology the administration is attempting to implement throughout the governmental structure. Note that in the case of PBS it embodies a form of revenue sharing benefiting the local stations at the expense of the central network. Now, revenue sharing of this kind is the Nixon administration's principal means of getting rid of the remnants of Lyndon Johnson's Great Society and facilitating its own takeover of the government bureaus.

The federal bureaucracies that have been in a client-provider relationship to the consumers of public services will be cut back seriously, and the funds will be given to cities and states, under the guise of a return to local autonomy. But local autonomy, of course, has nothing to do with it. What is actually taking place is the reconsolidation of power and authority over the local recipients of public services. For the individual citizen, this does not substitute a greater degree of freedom from previously existing federal domination. The only practical effect in power terms is to free the President to cut down the federal bureaucracy, and with it his ideological opposition in Washington.

At the same time, on the federal level, the President is expanding the traditional presidential powers enormously. That, to me, is the essence of the New Federalism, and I see the fate of public broadcasting as a laboratory example. Where power lies in licensing, instead of appropriations, it takes a different route but to the same end—as in the case of localism versus the commercial networks.

Now, that, it seems to me, is the real explanation of the Whitehead maneuvers. What the networks can expect is a series of end runs at every stage intended to accomplish the buildup of local domination of broadcasting. Maybe what the networks need to do is assemble our best constitutional mechanics in a new kind of research and development operation. For, in addition to those rather old-fashioned power plays by the Nixon administration, there is bound to be further popular demand for regulation built into the oncoming technology. My guess is that you are going to have to come up with a very, very different constitutional theory if you are to preserve any of the freedoms you have enjoyed under the First Amendment.

Since this exchange took place, the Watergate affair has come to a head, cutting down key figures in the White House inner circle, and discrediting the survivors, in a fashion that brings into question the efficacy of the grand Nixonian design sketched here by Harvey Wheeler. The sensational scandals that marked the opening months of the second term, however, do bear out Wheeler's view of the President's intent and his method. The childish cops-and-robbers invasion of Democratic headquarters was, in fact, as former Attorney General John Mitchell always described it, a silly business. The significant revelations came seriatim in the reaction of those who, under Mr. Nixon's dispensation, held places at the nerve center of executive power and exercised it with a ruthlessness and an arrogance not seen in Washington in the memory of the oldest observers.

Watergate was the perhaps inevitable product of the peculiarly conspiratorial cast of mind that characterizes the President and throughout his career has pushed him into extreme positions that run contrary to his surface reputation as a pragmatic wheeler-dealer. Surrounded, as he sees himself, by powerful forces plotting to undo him personally in order to subvert his shining vision of Middle America reincarnate, he has always deemed any political weapon justified by the venality of his enemies and the righteousness of his own cause. A man so beleaguered can survive only by exacting absolute fealty from the few who are allowed to penetrate his brooding loneliness and bear forth the fruit of his special inspiration.

It follows that those who fit these specifications could convince themselves that they constituted an interlocking circle impervious to onslaught from the Congress or the media, and, with their reach into the Department of Justice, immune to the ordinary working of the law. When the clumsy espionage effort in the reelection campaign blundered into public notice, the foreordained reaction was to buy up a few underlings and toss them to the official investigators, deny any knowledge or complicity by those directly associated with the President, and assiduously denigrate any who persisted in keeping the issue alive.

A typical sample of the protective tissue of categorical denials and outright lies is provided in this declaration by Clark McGregor, after he had been sent from the White House to succeed John Mitchell as head of the reelection committee: "Using innuendo, third-person hearsay, unsubstantiated charges, anonymous sources and huge scare headlines, the [*Washington*] *Post* has maliciously sought to give the appearance of a direct connection between the White House and the Watergate, a charge which the *Post* knows— and a half dozen other investigations have found—to be false."

The alarming fact is that this spurious construct came very close to remaining "operative," in the wonderful usage applied by Press Secretary Ronald Ziegler when he came to his own Gethsemane. It was blind luck of the draw that turned up in the federal court where the Watergate's living sacrifices were consigned a judge who would not tolerate the lackadaisical prosecution provided by the Justice Department and took matters into his own hands. There was, as it turned out, also much to be learned from sources uncovered by what started out to be a routine partisan effort to exploit the scandal through a civil damage suit brought by the Democratic National Committee. And finally the elders of the Senate rode into action, their sensibilities wounded by the cavalier treatment of the young men in the White House charged with carrying out the Nixonian design for expanding executive power at the expense of the legislative branch.

But I think it is fair to say that Watergate failed to slide into the oblivion planned for it primarily because a few stubborn journalists refused to accept the insult to their intelligence implicit in the administration's insistence that such an operation could have been undertaken independently of the most rigidly organized presidential entourage ever seen in Washington. All in all, the affair stands as an exemplary performance by national media carrying out the adversary role envisioned by the First Amendment.

It illustrates, too, how few are the news-gathering organizations with the capacity and the will for this kind of sustained confrontation. While there were significant contributions from individual journalists from major newspaper bureaus in Washington, the brunt was borne by the *Washington Post*, the *New York Times*, and the *Los Angeles Times*, with an intermittent effort by the three networks to put the bits and pieces together in a way that brought into question the "operative" fabrications set forth by the presidential surrogates.

It cannot be said that those on the front line always enjoyed support and approbation from the newspaper and broadcasting fraternity. In the early days, at least, it would be my guess that a substantial majority of local newspaper proprietors and station owners tended to accept the official view of Watergate as an insignificant "private eye caper," representing at worst an injudicious and excessive application of standard political campaign techniques. It followed that they would regard their embattled colleagues as embittered partisans or hopeless show-offs. The feeling carried over to the working press—compounded as always by professional jealousy of those who enjoy the high visibility that comes with the Washington political beat.

Physically located directly under the White House guns, and inheritor of an ancient enmity that goes back to Richard Nixon's tortured earlier years in the capital, the *Washington Post* earned the most numerous and varied collection of wound stripes in the course of the Watergate campaign. Official Washington is a small town within the larger city where the social scene is inseparable from the jousting within the corridors of power, and contact between adversaries is unavoidable. This makes possible certain personal cruelties and degradations—as when a women's page columnist for the *Post* was publicly insulted at a Nixon inaugural party by Frank Sinatra, the unlikely new boon companion of Vice-President Spiro Agnew.

This kind of thing may be written off as a normal hazard of the journalistic trade. I encountered it as executive editor of the *Arkansas Gazette*, when the newspaper was under siege during the long anti-integration campaign waged by the state government of Governor Orval Faubus. A poignant memory is of the dinner parties where the hostess would announce that for at least the duration of the meal "the subject" was off limits. This sometimes produced an interval of as much as ten minutes before two red-faced guests were straining across the table at each other. The moral may lie in the observation of Jonathan Daniels of the *Raleigh News and Observer* dynasty that we always do well to remember that in the end journalism is not a respectable business.

These surface lacerations, however, do not end with a simple exchange of unpleasantries. Paul Porter's recitation of the maneuvering involving political associates of the President and the Florida television licenses of the *Washington Post* is an indication of the manner in which the adversary procedure may move to the point where the flow of blood is not limited to that required to produce a flushed face. In the course of its confrontation with the White House, the value of the stock of the *Post*'s publishing corporation, which owns *Newsweek* as well as the newspaper and TV stations and is listed on the stock exchange, plunged at a rate that far exceeded the general market decline. The effect, of course, was to immediately pare the personal fortune of the *Post*'s president and publisher, Katherine Graham, and vastly complicate the existence of her business managers, who, as is usual in the communications industry, employ a financial statement as an essential tool of doing business.

The fact, then, is that as things now stand the people's right to know, as envisioned by the First Amendment, may turn on so fragile a human factor as the stamina of a bold editor like Benjamin Bradlee, backed by the integrity and commitment of an owner like Katherine Graham. These richly deserve the honors that have come to them, but their successful campaign at the Watergate cannot be isolated from the system in which they operate—but, unfortunately, do not typify.

# CHAPTER 7

# THE ALTERNATIVE
# TO REGULATION

I N 1815 John Adams concluded that finding an effective
means to regulate the press was the most difficult, dangerous, and important problem facing the new republic's
philosophers, theologians, legislators, politicians, and moral-
ists. "Mankind cannot now be governed without it," he
wrote, "nor at present with it."

More than a century later, when the technological imperatives of broadcasting finally pushed a reluctant government
into a regulatory stance, the men chosen to sit on the Federal
Communications Commission were still faced with the un-
resolved dilemma cited by the second president. As has been
seen, their legislative mandate was deliberately left ambigu-
ous; they were at once critics and accomplices of the new
broadcast industry; they were regulators, but they could not
be censors; the public tended to charge them with responsibility for the quality of a universal public service, and yet
the Commission was denied the rate-making and standard-
setting authority applied to public utilities by other regulatory agencies.

In the way of Washington, the range of commissioners has

been considerable. Some were political hacks looking for a sinecure; a good many were sincere but limited men who earned the accolade of the honky-tonk piano player spared shooting because he was doing the best he could; a few have been proved venal. But the Commission has usually had one or two outspoken members who have used their presumed independence to warn anyone who would listen that, in terms of the general welfare, the FCC's tangled proceedings are enormously significant, and grossly inadequate.

The Commission generally has been looked upon as more a handmaiden than a threat to the broadcasting industry. This, of course, follows the disheartening pattern of the nation's experience with regulatory agencies in general; the communications commissioners had ample precedent when their strictures against the regulatees rarely exceeded an avuncular reminder that such derelictions as excessive violence, neglectful or exploitative juvenile programming, intrusive commercials, and generally maintaining a vast intellectual wasteland weren't really in the best interests of the enterprise to which the Commission and the broadcasters shared a common devotion.

This cozy relationship was typified by Dean Burch, President Nixon's appointee as FCC chairman, when he appeared before the 1973 convention of the National Association of Broadcasters and warned the members that they had better act on their own to tone down "topless radio shows" providing "electronic voyeurism" for daytime audiences. Said the Chairman: "I am talking about three, four, five hours of titillating chitchat . . . on such elevated topics of urgent public concern as the number and frequency of orgasms, of the endless varieties of oral sex, or a baker's dozen other turn-ons, turn-offs, and turn-downs. . . . Do not, ladies and gentlemen, please do not permit the gamesmen and the schlock operators to call down on all your heads the open-ended and unpredictable consequences of their perverse folly." Failure to heed his warning, he suggested, could severely harm the industry's (and the administration's) effort to persuade Congress to extend broadcast license renewals from three to five years.

The effectiveness of this sort of stick-and-carrot censorship, at least in peripheral matters, was promptly demonstrated. The bellwether for the telephone colloquy between a *Playboy*-style interrogator and assorted suburban lonely-hearts was a Los Angeles personality syndicated by the Storer Broadcasting Company. Responding to Chairman Burch, Peter Storer, the chain's executive vice-president, announced that the Bill Ballance Feminine Forum would forthwith be completely restyled and would become simply the Bill Ballance Show—possibly without the telephone format, or in any case without the intimate topics that had won it a devoted following. The Ballance program's image, Storer said, had been "colored and damaged by less restricted imitators," and "rather than create added problems for broadcasting, we prefer to be responsive."

The most sustained and stringent criticism of this kind of back-scratching has come from Nicholas Johnson, an expatriate law professor from the University of California who quite properly assumed he would have no future with the FCC after the expiration of his term at the end of June 1973. It was the habit of this spirited maverick to express his low opinion of the broadcasting industry, and of his fellow commissioners, anywhere he could find a forum, including the hearings of the Senate and House committees charged with oversight of his agency. Here is a fair sample, addressed to Senator John Pastore of Rhode Island, the presiding elder on the Senate side:

A broadcasting license has, understandably, been characterized as a "license to print money." There is no question about the financial ability of this industry to provide the American people what the National Association of Broadcasters characterized in the early days as a "considerable proportion of programs devoted to . . . activities concerned with human betterment." Is television providing such a service? Is it serving "the public interest"? Virtually every independent critic has given the industry failing marks. Not only has the industry failed miserably in its great opportunity, and obligation, to contribute to "human betterment," it has actually done great harm.

Johnson was particularly infuriated by the broadcasters' standard defense against their critics. To point to high audience ratings as evidence that most of the public likes TV the way it is, he insisted, is to confuse the public interest with what interests the public, and even this is hardly valid, since the public's choice is limited by the sameness and repetition of standard TV fare. The proposition obviously serves the self-interest of an industry which, he has charged, "is not in the programming business, it is in the business of selling an audience to a merchandiser." He saw the end result as nullifying what he regarded as the mandate of the Communications Act to regulate broadcasting according to normative standards. In a last hurrah before yielding his seat on the Commission, he placed into the record a 264-page report, "Broadcasting in America," in which he and his staff ranked the 144 network-owned or -affiliated stations in the top fifty markets in order from best to worst.

Johnson did not attempt to pass judgment on the quality of program content, but based his performance criteria on the stations' own records as filed with the Commission in response to standards spelled out in FCC regulations for the issuance or renewal of a license: the amount of local programming, particularly in prime time; the amount of news, public affairs, and other informational material; the degree of restraint from overcommercialization as shown by frequency of advertising matter; and the ratio of gross income to program expenditure. For good measure, he included ratings on each station's percentage and category of minority and women employees.

"Most citizens," the Johnson valedictory concluded, "believe that broadcasters have an absolute right to program by whim, to present to millions of daily viewers whatever they might choose, in whatever sequence, at whatever time. . . . The law says just the opposite."

Johnson has long warned the broadcasters they were heading for disaster. He charged the hired spokesmen for the industry associations, and the sycophantic trade press, with "taking the broadcasters themselves—jovial, prosperous, martini-in-hand—down a jungle road into the largest ambush from an outraged citizenry ever unleashed upon an unsuspecting American industry." While the Commissioner could hardly be expected to applaud the advent of Richard Nixon as an avenging angel, he said of the complaints received by the Commission: "Areas of concern and levels of sophistication vary. But that television needs some improvement, and that the profiteers of the airways are not living up to their responsibilities, are propositions for which Vice-President Agnew's army and the 'effete intellectual snobs' can march arm in arm."

During his tenure on the FCC, Johnson let his hair grow long and deliberately identified himself with the counterculture. He can claim a legacy in the organized citizens groups he actively encouraged to bring public pressure, and, wherever possible, legal action, against broadcasters he considered errant. The Citizens Communications Center of Washington, D.C., provided co-counsel in the *BEM* case cited earlier, and legal assistance in the black coalition challenge to the Taft Broadcasting Corporation license in Columbus, Ohio, cited by Lawrence Rogers as an example of the "chamber of horrors" to which licensees can be subjected as a result of ascertainment procedures required by the federal bureaucrats. When the Rogers statement was published in *The Center Magazine*, CCC's executive director, Albert H. Kramer, cited it as evidence that the Conference on Broadcasting and the First Amendment had been dominated by the special interests of the industry and government at the expense of the popular interest, now represented—exclusively, he implied—by "thousands of citizens who have taken an active role in broadcasting regulation, who comprise a movement which has done more to make the broadcasting industry more responsive than any FCC or court decision."

The variety of internal conflicts of interest within the full range of telecommunication operations produces a constant struggle for advantage turning on actions not only by FCC but by a number of other government agencies. These essentially technical and economic considerations provided justification for the creation of the Office of Telecommunications Policy in the White House as the end product of a move toward affecting more effective coordination of the government's diverse communication activities begun under the Eisenhower administration. The Network Project's *Notebook on OTP* summarizes the rationale:

The government's dependence upon the communications industry as supplier of hardware and services is matched by the industry's reliance upon government as financier of telecommunications advances. In recent years, the federal government, largely through the Pentagon and NASA, has spent well over $50 billion for communications equipment, and billions more on research and development. The beneficiaries have been the new corporations in aerospace and electronics. Federal subsidies to these companies have so dramatically affected the economic ascendance of America's communications establishment that by 1971 nineteen electronics and aerospace firms were represented among the top twenty defense contractors. Their dependence upon the government's military and space establishment indicates a symbiotic arrangement which has had as great an impact on the country's communications environment as have the regulatory proceedings of the FCC. It is not surprising that administrations have moved to centralize management of this telecommunications structure, and sought to influence FCC policy to coincide with the government's own requirements and objectives.

Clay T. Whitehead came to OTP from an engineering and management background at the Massachusetts Institute of Technology and made a considerable impact upon the industry before he attracted public attention with his political foray against public and commercial network broadcasting. In a February, 1970, *Broadcasting* magazine interview he characterized his role as that of communications czar: "The White House has no qualms about seeking to influence the Commission (FCC) or other so-called independent agencies." In 1971, when the broadcasters protested proposed FCC rules on cable television, Whitehead assembled the interested parties, including FCC Chairman Dean Burch, in his OTP office and hammered out a compromise later embodied in FCC regulations. Nicholas Johnson charged that this procedure made a mockery of the Commission's presumed independence from influence by the executive branch, and in his dissenting opinion wrote:

"In future years, when students of law or government wish to study the decision-making process at its worst, when they look for examples of industry domination of government, when they look for presidential interference in the operation of an agency responsible to Congress, they will look to the FCC handling of the never-ending saga of cable television as a classical study. It is unfortunate, if not fatal, that the decision must be described in these terms, for of the national communications policy questions before us, none is more important to the country's future than cable television."

Even if Commissioner Johnson's testimony is discounted on partisan grounds, the conclusion still must be that in the light of a track record extending over nearly half a century, the federal effort at regulating—or overseeing—broadcasting has to be rated a failure at any significant point of conflict between the public's interest and that of the industry. The obvious lack of diversity in programming is the best evidence of the broadcasters' success in nullifying the equivalent of marketplace competition. This places a special burden upon those who accept the First Amendment as a valid proscription against direct government intervention. They are left with the necessity of inventing some novel, extralegal device which might somehow break through the pall of self-interest, timidity, and redundancy that produced this summary verdict from Jack Gould, the *New York Times* critic: "Television, to be blunt about it, is basically a medium with a mind closed to the swiftly moving currents of tomorrow. The networks have erected an electronic wall around the status quo."

Perhaps the most ambitious move in that direction was undertaken in 1947 by a private Commission on the Freedom of the Press financed by the late Henry Luce of Time, Inc., and chaired by Robert M. Hutchins, then president of the University of Chicago. The commission, made up of scholars and public men who would have qualified for most lists of elder statesmen, called for creation of a permanent body to exercise oversight of the performance of the media and regularly report its findings to the public.

The Hutchins group recommended a wholly private agency to be financed by foundations and made up of distinguished citizens of high character, demonstrated competence, and total detachment from any current financial dependence upon the communications industry. Its mission would be to render periodic appraisals of the performance of the media under the criteria their proprietors profess to set for themselves. Newspapers, magazines, and radio (it is hard to believe, but 1947 was pre-television) would be judged on their capacity to provide (1) a truthful, comprehensive, and intelligent account of the day's events in a context which gives them meaning; (2) a forum for the exchange of comment and criticism; (3) the projection of a representative picture of the constituent groups in the society; (4) the presentation and clarification of the goals and values of the society; and (5) full access to the day's intelligence.

The proposal was all but unanimously rejected by the media, and the Hutchins Commission was roundly denounced. It was generally argued that any form of oversight and accountability somehow violated the spirit of the First Amendment and paved the way for government intervention in the affairs of the free press, which was precisely what the proposal did not do and, in fact, sought to avoid. Prophetically, the commission warned that "those who direct the machinery of the press have engaged from time to time in practices which the society condemns and which, if continued, it will inevitably undertake to regulate or control."

These arguments were revived in late 1972 by the Twentieth Century Fund's announcement that it had put together philanthropic support for a new Council on Press Responsibility and Press Freedom. Under a design somewhat more modest than that embodied in the earlier proposal, its operating arm, the National News Council, will limit its surveillance to the principal "wholesale" suppliers of news—the wire services, the networks, the syndicates, the supplemental services of the major newspapers, and national news magazines. It will follow the practice of the British Press Council, receiving complaints about specific cases of media performance, investigating, and publicly reporting its findings.

William L. Rivers, the Stanford communications expert, found that within two weeks after announcement of the new proposal he had collected "enough savage editorials about the Council to paper the walls of my office." The conservative *New York Daily News* charged a "sneak attempt at press regulation, a bid for a role as unofficial news censor." A. M. Rosenthal, managing editor of the liberal *New York Times*, expressed fear that such a body would in fact endanger press freedom, focus attention unduly on the shortcomings of the media, and become a loudspeaker for pressure groups "skilled in the methods of political propaganda." The 405 members who responded to a poll by the American Society of Newspaper Editors on the establishment of such a press council by ASNE were opposed three to one, and the opposition rose to four to one against a commission established by any other organization. Among the major broadcasters, only Richard Salant of CBS came forward with an unqualified endorsement.

At the Center conference, Roger Traynor, the retired Chief Justice of the California Supreme Court, who will serve as founding chairman of the Twentieth Century Fund project, discussed the theory and practice of private oversight with the obviously divided participants.

TRAYNOR: I was very interested in Lord Ritchie-Calder's reply when he was asked whether the esteem of the media in Great Britain is higher than it is in this country. I am curious as to how much the establishment of the British Press Council had to do with that. Despite its earlier opposition, I understand the press in Britain is now quite enthusiastic in its support.

RITCHIE-CALDER: Eighty-five percent of all editors now approve of the Council. Mark you, that includes some people I wouldn't join a club with . . .

TRAYNOR: Well, I hope we can establish a similar record, but that remains to be seen. The press council idea has always encountered opposition here, and I have been made aware that this is still the case. I confess that I do not understand most of the criticism we are receiving. Our basic purpose is best stated in our charter: "The National News Council is a private and independent institution, established to serve the public interest in preserving freedom of communication." The major premise underlying that phrase is that the news media are not the only ordained guardians and protectors of freedom of the press. The public has a deep interest here, entirely aside from the interest of those who are engaged in the communications business.

We also are charged "with advancing accurate and fair reporting of news; to affirm the values of freedom of expression in a democratic society; to promote public understanding of those values, and the responsibility of the public as well as the media for their preservation; to initiate research and issue reports on these matters; and to provide an open and independent forum to receive and investigate complaints on accuracy, and to consider complaints by members of the media concerning the conduct of individuals and organizations toward the nation's major print and electronic media."

When we are fully established, we will have fifteen members, nine public members chosen for eminence and prestige and demonstrated impartiality and objectivity, and six members associated with the media, but who are not owners or employees of the national media, which we are charged with overseeing. When there is a meeting of the Council to hear a complaint by a person against the media, or a complaint by the media against a person, either private or public, those meetings are to be open, which of course means subject to coverage by the media. The Council will receive no information in confidence.

Prior to a public hearing, however, we will have determined whether or not to hear the complaint. There will be a screening to eliminate crackpot charges. Our other function, which I think may turn out to be even more important, is to conduct studies on incursions against freedom of the press, to see how that freedom can be protected and preserved.

ASHMORE: If the Council had been in being when Whitehead's speech burst upon the public consciousness, would it have been expected to make any kind of response on its own motion?

TRAYNOR: We'd certainly study the implications, investigate, and have a hearing if that were in order, and make a report.

PORTER: Suppose Whitehead wouldn't appear?

TRAYNOR: Well, we can't make anybody appear. The Council has no subpoena power. I would expect that those who do not cooperate might seem conspicuous by their absence.

ASHMORE: That means you would have accepted an obligation to try to clarify the ambiguities that have been raised in the course of these discussions? The Council would reach some kind of judgment on what Mr. Whitehead really meant and what the effect might be?

TRAYNOR: I think that would have been a very appropriate and proper function for the Council. This is why I am puzzled as to why this proposal should have met such widespread opposition from the news media. Our discussions here seem to me to demonstrate the value of such a Council. As we establish procedures for the fair hearing of complaints against the media, we will also establish procedures whereby the media can bring complaints against any person, public or private. One vital condition is a stipulation that those on both sides will forgo legal or administrative action. We are determined to protect ourselves against being used as a pretrial discovery device by lawyers to collect evidence to be used later in litigation.

PORTER: How would you prevent that, Justice Traynor? If somebody wants to challenge a TV station license on the grounds of something your Council had found in relation to that station's public affairs programming, how would you keep him from doing that?

TRAYNOR: Well, we wouldn't hear his case—

PORTER: You would stipulate that he would not use your findings in action on a license renewal?

TRAYNOR: That's right. He would have to stipulate that first. And there's also a stipulation that there can be no action for libel against anybody who appears before this Council . . .

PORTER: Would the courts respect those stipulations?

RITCHIE-CALDER: Similar requirements are written into the charter of the British Press Council, and I recall no problems.

SEVAREID: But how do you prevent someone who was not a party to the Council hearing from using your findings to prove that a broadcast license should not be renewed? You couldn't stop that, could you?

TRAYNOR: You mean, stop litigation?

SEVAREID: No. Suppose you have made a public finding that some broadcaster has not lived up to his obligation. How would you prevent that public record from being introduced by someone who wanted to take over the license?

TRAYNOR: There might be a danger in that. I don't think so, though.

SALANT: Let me say that in the course of our consideration of the possibilities of this procedure, this was the most troublesome question so far as broadcasting was concerned. I was on the task force that recommended Justice Traynor's News Council, and we gave much attention to the possibility that its adverse findings would in some way be incorporated into FCC action, and so take on an official coloration. There are two protections against that. One is that this procedure is entirely voluntary. I take the position that the minute any broadcast organization that has been responding to complaints addressed to the News Council finds that it is placing itself in official jeopardy, all it needs to do is bow out. Second, representatives of the task force discussed the problem with the FCC, and got a commitment—legally worth the paper it was written on, I guess—that the Commission would respect the conditions set by the Council.

PORTER: Suppose Station A has been clobbered by the News Council. Applicant B comes in and jumps Station A's license, and he says at a full evidential hearing, "I want to introduce the findings of the News Council that Station A has not carried out its public responsibilities." What examiner would refuse to hear that?

SALANT: Any sensible examiner would refuse to hear it, or at least take into account that, by gosh, here is a broadcaster who was conscientious enough to look for a second opinion when he was accused of wrongdoing.

CUTLER: There are other reasons, Paul. I think you have to take as a given that the complaint against A's conduct would still be in existence, unadjudicated, if this Council had never passed on it. It would be there and available to be litigated in the FCC forum. If the media council had acted on the complaint, the chances are, looking at the British experience, that if it was without merit it would have been rejected. In that case, it might be the licensed station wanting to bring up the fact that the News Council had vindicated its operation.

PORTER: Would you advise a client under attack before the News Council to respond if you felt that his license would be in jeopardy in the event of an adverse decision?

CUTLER: Yes, I would. Because under those circumstances his license might be in even greater jeopardy if he didn't respond.

ASHMORE: If your client is guilty, and you know him to be, doesn't he have a chance to get cleaned up by voluntarily going before the Council?

CUTLER: Yes. He has the opportunity, if the Council has made an adverse finding, to do something about it, and show that he has done so before the official hearing on his license comes up.

RITCHIE-CALDER: It seems to me that what Judge Traynor is really getting at is what Mr. Salant was asking for, a practical means of "rewriting" the First Amendment to provide a bill of rights for broadcasters.

ROBERT HUTCHINS: I would like to emphasize something Ritchie-Calder said earlier. I was in England at the time the original proposal for the British Press Council was made, and since I was coincidentally chairman of the American Commission on a Free and Responsible Press, I was asked to be the first witness before the Royal Commission. It was perfectly clear that nobody wanted a press council. I was told that Mr. Attlee, the Prime Minister, didn't want the Royal Commission to bring forth a favorable report. J. B. Priestley resigned after a very few meetings.

I am sure that in the first five years of the British Press Council, any serious effort to abolish it would have succeeded. Then the personnel changed. Lord Devlin was put in as a firm and prestigious chairman, other lay members were added, and the Council really began to face up to some important questions about the press. There followed a degree of popularity that was absolutely unbelievable as of the day the original Council was established.

The answer to Justice Traynor's question about the present

reception of his Council is that it doesn't make much difference. I have no doubt those reservations will disappear as your work goes on and begins to command the respect of the groups which should be supporting it now.

CUTLER: I think the reason the British Council won acceptance is because the instinct of the best newspaper owners, television network owners, and I think station owners, maybe to a lesser degree, is toward professionalism. The best of them have pride in the professional public service aspects of journalism . . .

PORTER: Lloyd, that's the reason they say they don't want anybody looking over their shoulders.

CUTLER: But that's not a problem for those who understand that there is no real conflict between their duty to serve the public and their desire to make money. There is plenty of evidence to show that the surest way for an owner to make money is to be a good, professional journalist. That will earn him public respect, and the profits from the show-business aspect of broadcasting will follow. Dick Salant is not dissembling when he cites the lack of pressure from advertisers on his news operation. I have worked for enough auto companies and chemical companies and others who have been, they think, vilified in the news, to be sure that they get nowhere by waving their advertising contracts at Frank Stanton and William Paley of CBS. A press council that applies standards of professional journalism should have no trouble convincing professional journalists that they have nothing to fear, and may have something to gain.

Although the first reaction within the media to the announcement of the National News Council was negative, there is some indication that this automatic reflex may be diminishing as the proposal becomes better understood. From the outset some of the country's most respected newspapers endorsed the proposal, among them the *Denver Post, Cleveland Plain Dealer, Milwaukee Journal, Louisville Courier-Journal, St. Louis Post-Dispatch,* and *Dayton News.* With the backing of CBS, the record among the networks was one for, two against.

Laurence I. Barrett, writing in the Columbia University *Journalism Review,* found the most ominous portent in *New York Times* publisher Adolf Ochs Sulzburger's formal announcement that "we will not be a party to Council investigations. We will not furnish information or explanations to the Council. In our coverage we will treat the Council as we treat any other organization; we will report their activities when they are newsworthy." The *Times,* as Barrett pointed out, is one of the principal "national wholesalers of news" to whom the Council would address its attention, while the newspapers listed among its supporters are regional, and presumably exempt from challenge before the Council. Although none has gone as far as the *Times,* three other national news suppliers reacted negatively, the *Wall Street Journal,* the *Washington Post,* and the *Los Angeles Times.*

Coverage of the announcement of the News Council's formation was spotty. Among the newspapers, magazines, and networks that would be affected, Barrett found, "there was a large volume of quiet. For the press council, no news is bad news indeed. Lacking any kind of police power or institutional status, it can succeed only if it builds some moral authority, as its British model has done. And that can happen only if the organizations covered give it some degree of recognition, even if the recognition is in some cases hostile. Clearly, that is not what is happening."

There is, however, evidence of high-level internal policy

division among the affected media. At the *New York Times,* John Oakes, the editorial page editor and a member of the owning family, was a member of the Twentieth Century Fund task force and continues to support the proposal in principle. At the *Washington Post,* Benjamin Bradlee, the executive editor, doubts that the Council will work but seems indisposed to withhold cooperation.

This cleavage extends even into the ranks of journalism professors. Anonymous editorial comment in the *Columbia Journalism Review* criticized the News Council because it set its sights well below those of the old Hutchins Commission, and concluded: "The Council may do no obvious harm and it might do some public relations good. But in the longer term, does its existence not present a danger that the public will believe it is getting something that it is not?" An editorial note was appended dissociating the *Review*'s editor, Alfred Balk, who served as rapporteur for the Twentieth Century Fund task force and wrote its summary report, *A Free and Responsive Press.*

George Reedy, former press secretary to President Johnson and now dean of Marquette University's journalism school, opposes the News Council in principle but believes its time may have come. Reedy goes back to the findings of the earlier Hutchins Commission to make the point that, while the ambitions and aberrations of Richard Nixon and his men may have brought the issue to a new climax, the real pressures toward government intervention are the product of systemic change and exist without regard to the political fortunes of any incumbent president. He identifies and endorses this warning as the basic finding of the prior commission:

"No democracy, certainly not the American democracy, will indefinitely tolerate concentration of private power irresponsible and strong enough to thwart the aspirations of the people. Eventually governmental power will be used to regulate private power—if private power is at once great and irresponsible. Our society requires agencies of mass communication. They are great concentrations of private power. If they are irresponsible, not even the First Amendment will protect their freedom from governmental control. The Amendment will be amended."

The parallel with the British experience is striking. Lord Ritchie-Calder, in a background paper for the Center conference, recalled that as a working journalist he personally shared the opposition to the Press Council when it was launched twenty-five years ago:

I thought it a kangaroo court, with no proper status or sanctions. But mainly I opposed it because, defaulting from the recommendations of the Royal Commission, it included no lay members. It consisted of twenty-five newspapermen—ten from the managerial level and fifteen from the editorial staffs. The chairman was a columnist. The results were derisory; editors would refuse to appear or recognise the existence of the tribunal or acknowledge its findings.

Subsequently, the Council was reorganised. Five professional places were dropped and ten laymen were included. Lord Devlin, a forthright judge respected by the press, became chairman. He was a lay member, but his invisible wig and gown gave the body a paralegal appearance. His successor, Lord Pearce, is a former Appeals Judge. Although they can't be compelled to publish their own indictments and the strictures of the Council, this new eminence is such that only twice in recent years has a newspaper failed to publish findings critical of its conduct.

The Council selects the cases on which it will adjudicate. About one in four complaints are "tried." The rest will have been rejected as "frivolous." Others will be rejected where legal action has been initiated or threatened or where the proper recourse is to the judicial courts. In 1971, of 38 cases adjudicated only 13 complaints were upheld.

The Council, without legal sanctions, tends to be regarded by the litigious complainant as an unsatisfying tribunal. However, the "toothless" judgments carry some real weight. In the summary of facts and findings, the editor of the offending publication is held responsible but the individual journalist guilty of unprofessional conduct, of invasions of privacy, or of "bad taste" will be named.

The Council's judgments consist of two kinds: an admonition or a censure. Although the penalties are no more than a slap on the wrist, or the public pillory, the newspaper professionals no longer are derisory.

The Council has on occasion uttered very strong strictures on the general tendencies of the press—underscoring a non-existent rubric of professional conduct. It has also effectively spoken out in cases of unjustified harassment and has taken the part of journalists against editors in the handling of stories, or pressures to unethical conduct, or against unfair criticism or attack by readers.

Justice Traynor is unflappable and forthright, and like Lord Devlin and Lord Pearce he still wears an invisible judicial gown, if not a wig. In response to the *New York Times* pledge of non-cooperation, he said simply, "I do not believe that the *Times* would refuse to publish the Council's findings even if they were against the *Times* . . ." And in a statement published in *The Center Magazine* he said of Sulzberger's expressed "fear that [the Council] would encourage an atmosphere of regulation in which government intervention might gain public acceptance":

I think that the Council can be a buffer between government and the press. If it is true that the media are held in low esteem by the public, the Council might be able to expose the reasons for that low esteem.

If the media have been inaccurate or unfair, why should they be immune from criticism? If a person has been aggrieved, why should his grievance not be exposed and redressed at least to the extent that the findings of an impartial and reputable body, dedicated to fairness and objectivity, are given publicity? Why should the media not be vindicated when they are unfairly attacked?

I cannot believe that the Council, completely detached from government and without any power to impose any sanctions whatever other than publicity, can be in any way a threat to press freedom or can encourage an atmosphere of regulation. What have the media to fear from publicity, their very stock in trade? Are they so infallible as to be above criticism? Must the defense of freedom of the press be left solely to them?

I see no risk whatever that the News Council would encourage government intervention. Indeed, it would do the opposite by serving to remove any basis for any claim that there is a need for such intervention. The risk is rather that government officials might otherwise be encouraged to attack the assumption of media infallibility, on which opposition to news councils seems to be based, and to exploit public disaffection with the media.

# CHAPTER 8

# "THE ONLY
# SOLID BASIS . . ."

JOURNALISM has come a long way since it took form as the product of the enterprise and the passion of men who set their own type and hawked their opinions on the street. Today, in its most influential manifestation, it is a prestigious but expensive and troublesome appendage to an industry designed primarily to provide popular entertainment and promote the sale of goods and services. In that exposed position the flow of news and opinion is dependent not only upon the integrity of practicing broadcast journalists, but upon the personal commitment of proprietors and managers acting in response to a sense of public obligation, or at least to a desire for a different kind of status and influence than can be acquired by simply amassing wealth.

The founding generation of broadcast barons is about gone. General David Sarnoff of NBC is dead; Frank Stanton no longer stands at the right hand of William Paley of CBS, and ABC is headed by an import from the theater business. There is reason to believe, in any case, that these huge communications conglomerates have grown past the point where they can be subjected to the personal imprint of any one man. The journalists who fashion their national and international news services wage their daily contest with space and time in the far corners of vast bureaucratic hives, which add to the ancient frustrations the cautious pace of policy-making by committee.

The record of broadcast journalism to date has been better than its circumstances give us any right to expect. The sins are primarily of omission, and there have been many moments of glory made possible by those before the cameras and behind the scenes who stubbornly held to their commitment to truth—or, as Richard Salant would have it, to fairness, which is about all any journalist can aspire to in a calling that deals primarily with contingent facts. But there too the guard is changing; the veteran reporters and commentators who came to the medium conditioned by the older newspaper tradition are giving way to charismatic newcomers who have known only the team effort and show-business trappings of electronic journalism. There is no place here for a lonely iconoclast, but there is plenty of room at the top for handsome young persons seeking wealth and celebrity of an order working journalists have never known before.

The over-all change in the pattern of mass communications represents a quantum jump that may prove to be as profound in its ultimate social consequences as Gutenberg's introduction of movable type. Television has extended human communication into dimensions beyond those accepted for centuries as absolute physical limits. We still know very little about the sensory impact of these airborne signals upon the recipient's perception, and upon his psyche. However, the more mundane aspects of the primacy gained by the electronic media in the last decade are now acknowledged by the accountants who measure the economic base of the communications structure.

In sum, the tendency so far has been toward consolidation of control rather than toward diversity and innovation. Despite diminishing technological restraints, the doctrine of scarcity has survived as the basis for a national broadcasting system that permits concentration of the bulk of programming in the hands of three giant profit-making corporations. The new competition for the advertising dollar has produced a great shakeout in the print media. In the face of the urban growth patterns of the last three decades, we had in 1973 exactly the same number of daily newspapers, 1,749, we had at the end of World War II. Most of these claim local market monopoly as essential to their survival, and the contraction of ownership is such that only New York still supports more than two daily newspaper managements. All the great general readership magazines, which for almost a century enjoyed the only national circulation among the print media, have fallen before the electronic newcomer. At the wake for the last survivor, *Life*, which succumbed in December, 1972, one of the managerial mourners offered this epitaph: "We were doomed when news pictures began to move."

After an initial surge of experimentation with new journalistic forms suitable to the visual medium, television has lapsed into the stereotypes that for a decade have characterized network news programming: the solid, straightforward anchor man (Cronkite, Chancellor, Reasoner) sketching in the hard news; an urbane (Sevareid) or acerbic (Brinkley) or earnest (Smith) commentator providing three minutes and twenty seconds of perspective; and in between terse messages from reporters in the field, who are most likely to turn up in semi-mod dress, microphone in hand, reading a hurried summary of what just happened in a back-lit White House, Kremlin, Capitol, Statehouse, or City Hall, or performing voice-over while the camera pans the site of some non-political disaster.

This early-evening half hour of tightly fabricated news is by no means representative of the total output of the highly competent network staffs, which also supply sustenance for the morning shows, the weekend backgrounders, the supercoverage of political conventions, assassinations, and moon shots, the "magazine format" programs, and the often distinguished documentaries which have a unique capacity for depicting great social issues in human terms. Still, the "evening news" dominates the scene, serving as the showcase for the total network news effort, and providing the critical standing in competitive ratings, which allocate the total audience of 60 million among the three. In the eyes of management it is these percentage points that more or less justify the remainder of the news and public affairs undertaking—which over all is not self-sustaining, and has to be written off to promotion and good will.

At the Center conference Eric Sevareid characterized the half-hour news format as a kind of Iron Maiden which forces upon all three networks a foreordained sameness in the selection and coverage of the day's major events. Within that narrow temporal limit there is almost no opportunity to get outside the news budget made mandatory by journalism's professional canons—the death of a great man; the threat of a new war or the day-by-day continuation of an old one; the advent or result of an election; a conspicuous action by a ruler or his mass opposition; a spectacular crime; or an act of God. The network news directors and commentators may alter the order and change the emphasis, but they display no more disposition to depart from the hard-core selection dictated by standardized news judgment than do the editors who decide the front-page makeup of the nation's newspapers. Sevareid put it this way:

We are all in the same bind. We've each got twenty-three, twenty-four minutes net, so we're bound to come out much alike in terms of news content. The real internal enemy of this business is not really bias, however you define that, it is haste and the terrible compression of material.

A lot of us have tried for a long time to see if we couldn't get the evening network shows up to an hour, and if we had succeeded I believe a lot of the pressure would have gone out of the boiler long before Agnew spoke out. With more time we could put on commentators of different persuasions, if that is what is wanted—and of course there would be room for rebuttals. Fifteen years ago a psychiatrist identified our Achilles' heel when he said the trouble with broadcasting is that people can't talk back to that little box.

When you pick up a newspaper, you are to some degree your own editor—you can roam around and decide what you want to read and ignore the rest. In broadcasting we are caught in linear time. To a local viewer the bus accident he just saw at Fourth and Main may deserve as much prominence as the outbreak of world war, but he can't do anything about it—and he feels trapped and restless.

Some aspects of this are beyond us. But if we were able to enlarge the scope of the programming—and let me concede that this is the result of the networks' decision, not anybody else's—I think a lot of things could be included that would relieve this feeling of compression. This might even include the so-called good-news stories, many of which are in fact real news. But when you sit down in that bear pit with news pouring in from all over the world, from so many sources, you have so little time—so few hours to make up your own mind, and a whole set of professional priorities you can't ignore.

If the ironbound half hour still prevails at the networks, the limitation has been dramatically lifted for local news. In

Los Angeles two of the three network-owned stations have expanded the news hold to two and one-half hours—two hours gross of locally originated matter, plus the half hour from the network. The reason for this is that spot advertising can be assembled around local programming so as to turn a profit, plus the consideration that these transitional hours into prime time may influence audience distribution throughout the evening. The immediate effect of this decompression has been to trivialize the local offering by putting new emphasis on light, inconsequential "human interest" features and intramural chitchat, if for no other reason than that there simply isn't enough hard local news to meet the presumed visual requirements of the TV format.

Inevitably, this process serves to enhance the show-business aspects of broadcast news, increasing the value of personality as opposed to journalistic skills—a condition reflected in the fact that top-rated Los Angeles anchor men command show-business incomes in excess of $100,000 a year. Once news content becomes secondary, merchandising takes over, and this is as true of the competition for audience ratings and advertising dollars in Washington, D.C.— long considered the journalistic capital of the world—as it is in Hollywood. Appraising the three leading local news shows, Tom Dowling wrote in the *Washington Star-News:* "Viewed purely as news packages, the differences between WRC, WMAL, and WTOP are negligible. . . . All three news shows suffer from manpower limitations and the high costs of running film crews." Each of these productions recognizes Washington's demography with a tandem pair of anchor men, one black and one white, and Dowling found the only real competition confined to heavy advertising and promotion campaigns devoted to building up these six personalities:

"Yes, out of the Great American Tradition that gave us

Carter's Little Liver Pills, LS/MFT, cures without end for animated stomach acid and tired blood, the Pepsi Generation, and even the new, improved Richard M. Nixon, comes the packaging and merchandising of Max & Gordon, Fred Thomas and Wes Sarginson, Rinker & Vance . . . Ah, a choice for every taste! Anchor men you can address by first name, complete name, or surname; news that's not just a drab recital of the day's events, but news with a unique angle . . . 'the best news you'll get all day,' news that 'gets into where you live,' and 'news that cares about people.'"

A few of the old-timers around the newsrooms seemed mildly embarrassed to find themselves served up in newspaper ads and billboards with such sudsy prose, but none felt disposed to protest. Glenn Rinker, the white half of the team at Washington's NBC-owned station, told Dowling:

"After six years on the show I already had a good public recognition factor. Now I can't even go into the supermarket without being recognized. Why, we're the same as show-biz people. A good anchor man has to have a show-biz style. You have to change moods and add a certain amount of dramatic quality to what you do on the air. . . . So if the station wants to use me, so what? If you don't like being used on TV, then you're in the wrong business. If you're an anchor man you're a superstar; it's inevitable. Why, people walk up to me on the streets and say, 'My wife is in love with you.' These promos are an ego thing, but what's wrong with that?"

In journalistic terms, the effect of this kind of localism in news reporting, as Richard Salant observed, makes no sense at all, since it allocates two hours to covering, if that is still the word, a single city, while trying to cram the record of the world and the nation into one-fourth that time. Add to this the trivializing factor, and there is no reason to challenge David Brinkley's reaction to the National Association of

Broadcasters' proud claim of preeminence in news and public affairs: "If most of the people in this country are getting most of their news from television, they are getting damned little news."

It probably is quite literally true that broadcasting, still in its technological infancy, is permanently trembling on the brink of some mechanical breakthrough that might galvanize the industry. Internally, this may come with the advent of new, lighter, more sensitive camera equipment. Richard C. Wald, successor to Reuven Frank as president of NBC News, has predicted that miniaturized, highly portable video equipment in the PCB 90 series due to come into service in 1973 will revolutionize news programming.

"The PCB," Wald said, "will change the form of what you see on the news—but I can't predict exactly how. Maybe, with its 'instant remote' capability, it will take us back to the earlier days of TV, when the news was sloppy and less reliable but hot off the griddle."

Coming up, Wald said, is a new system of videotape recording which will replace the present cumbersome cameras with a unit comparable to an ordinary record player, coupled to editing equipment that will give TV the speed and flexibility of radio. "Right now, when we go out on a story, it's like a newspaper reporter having to drag along a linotype machine. With the ability to phone in a video story from any telephone, you'd even be able to have an all-day news station."

But here, as with every technological breakthrough in the past, the problem may not turn on achieving wider and speedier access to the day's events, but on figuring out how to give them meaning. "If we confuse news with truth," Walter Lippmann wrote many years ago, "we will get nowhere." Now past eighty and still the country's preeminent journalistic philosopher, Lippmann said of the media's contest with the Nixon administration:

"I think very often the troubles of the press come from a commercialized desire to get scoops, to be the first to print the news. The desire . . . to be first to [publish] particular information is corrupting to the whole journalistic process. . . . I think raw news, raw fact, is not intelligible, anyway, to the public, and has to be explained. The explanation is as important as the fact itself. The duty of the press is to put forth not raw news, but explained news."

Over all, the newspapers generally have increased their quota of "explained news" in response to the electronic competition's successful inroads on the spot-news market. But TV can fully perform this function only within the broad limits of major news documentaries, and these have been declining in both quantity and quality. An appraisal of the 1971–72 broadcast season by Patrick D. Maines and John C. Ottinger in the *Columbia Journalism Review* found that the three networks combined had mustered the men and money to produce only fifty-one programs of one-half hour to two-hour duration under their own documentary classification. This once-a-week average was established in a national political campaign season which confronted TV with the quadrennial challenge of giving focus and perspective to the polemics of contending partisans. Yet only sixteen of these documentaries were devoted to any of the commanding issues developed in the presidential contest: war, inflation/ unemployment, crime/drug abuse, poverty/welfare, and busing/race. Maines and Ottinger summarized the season:

The relatively small attention paid to the season's most commanding issues—and the total absence of any documentary on two of them, inflation/unemployment and poverty/welfare—underscores the networks' most critical shortcoming: questionable relevance. For all the networks' resources and opportunities, and for all that can be said on behalf of non-issue documentaries, far too few documentaries of critical importance were produced and broadcast. . . .

Perhaps for reasons of "economics" too many issue-oriented documentaries were relegated to the end-of-season doldrums from June to September, when audiences are at their seasonal lows. Of its total of five documentaries on the major issues, ABC aired four in the June–September period. Two of NBC's four came after May 21. CBS did better; only two of its seven appeared during the summer slump.

There are still enough instances of the networks' tackling genuinely controversial issues to relieve them of suspicion that simple timidity is eroding the documentary form. For example, CBS went head on into the subject of TV advertising and had guts enough to name the major advertisers who refused to discuss questions of taste and accuracy with network reporters. Yet, while it was hardly a program intended to gain favor with those from whom advertising revenue must flow, the veteran broadcaster Maury Green wrote in the *Los Angeles Times:* "The program's only real flaw was that it barely touched the periphery of its fascinating subject: the hidden messages which TV transmits—messages wondrously sent and received without the conscious knowledge of either sender or receiver. Most of TV is like this. TV is the inferential medium; it communicates by viewer inference, without much regard for the message supposedly sent out."

Green cited the finding of sociologists that TV unconsciously produced the primary driving force behind the black protest movement with its glowing commercials showing the goods readily available to middle-class whites but beyond the reach of blacks, thus ironically coupling a "revolution of rising expectations" to an effort to peddle Pablum. Green reported that all three networks have rejected proposals for TV documentaries examining, scientifically, exactly how TV communicates via the subconscious, and added: "It would be interesting to know whether they themselves don't know, or don't want it known, or just don't give a damn."

If the network news operations have chosen to ignore what Green calls the inferential quality of TV, this is not true of the new breed of professional political managers who have come on the scene with the communications revolution. Their prime stock in trade is the special, manipulative potential of what one of the leading practitioners, Joseph Napolitan, calls the "instant information" provided by television and radio; this impact creates instant, visceral involvement on the part of the recipient, and if this takes place in a context controlled by a creative media expert the involvement can be translated into visceral support for a political candidate.

Back in 1964, when he was working as a media consultant in the Lyndon Johnson campaign, Napolitan discovered a self-made electronics genius named Tony Schwartz, who earns a handsome living fabricating radio and television commercials in a gadget-filled pair of joined town houses he inhabits on the west side of Manhattan. Out of that association came Schwartz's first political ad, destined to become one of the most famous, and least exposed, TV spots ever made. It ran thirty seconds and showed a little girl counting backward as she plucked petals from a daisy. A man's voice came on and took over the countdown: ". . . four, three, two, one." Bang. Silence, signifying the end of the world. Then the familiar voice of Lyndon Johnson: "We must learn to love each other, or die."

The commercial appeared only once, at 10 P.M. EST on NBC's *Monday Night at the Movies,* and that single exposure created such a violent reaction from the Republicans that the Democrats inferentially agreed it hit below the belt by withdrawing it. Four years later, when Napolitan was managing the media campaign for Hubert Humphrey, the memory of the backlash was so intense that the Democrats refused to release a similar Schwartz creation. This one shows the inside of a voting booth, with a hesitant hand reaching for the voting lever. There are three choices: Nixon-Agnew, Humphrey-Muskie, Wallace-LeMay. When the hand finally pulls the Wallace-LeMay lever, the booth disappears in an atomic shower.

Schwartz, an unabashed disciple of Marshall McLuhan, affects not to understand this squeamishness. The approach, in his view, simply employs the visual medium for its maximum persuasive potential—which, he points out, is what all campaign techniques, from the stump speech forward, are about. As to ethics, he contends that his daisy commercial was "one of the most moral statements ever delivered on television." He even suggests what he considers a totally effective countertactic: since the only attack was by inference, the Republicans could have neutralized the impact by endorsing the sentiment expressed by President Johnson and offering to pay half the cost of running the commercial on the networks for the remainder of the campaign.

The inferential approach was again epitomized in a Schwartz classic in the 1968 Democratic campaign, a radio commercial which opened with the steady bump-de-bump of a heart beating, louder, louder, louder. One of those sympathetic announcer's voices comes on: "Who do you want a heartbeat away from the presidency?" Pregnant pause. "Agnew . . . or Muskie?" Although Napolitan, with a more or less straight face, argues that this could be seen as an anti-

Muskie ad, it is obvious that in context the Republicans could not have endorsed it without emphasizing an issue they were trying to bury, the fitness of the potential presidential successor.

James M. Perry, analyzing the Schwartz technique in *The National Observer*, wrote: "There is a common thread running through all of these commercials. Each is stark, simple. None openly supports anyone or attacks anyone. It is the viewer who supplies the emotion. The viewer becomes involved, instantly and viscerally. It is pure McLuhan."

The candidates, who are generally old-line political practitioners likely to be issue-oriented (print-oriented, Schwartz would contemptuously substitute), so far have tended to restrain the hired media managers. However, the trend is clearly in this direction. The evidence suggests that Richard Nixon and his handlers are already converts, and have applied the Schwartz dicta in seeing to it that the President rarely is exposed on the media except under totally controlled circumstances. This, of course, is the great advantage of paid advertising, and an incumbent President is unique among politicians in enjoying its equivalent without cost while exercising his ceremonial duties as chief of state. Perry found the Schwartz formula working perfectly as the crippled Apollo 13 limped home from its journey into space:

The country stopped as the drama unfolded. No sooner had the astronauts dropped safely into the Pacific than President Nixon boarded a jet and scurried to Hawaii to welcome them. Radio reported his trip breathlessly. TV showed him there, basking in reflected glory. Newspapers, as instantly as possible, carried banner headlines. The President placed himself in the center of the drama. Information was conveyed. Instant reaction. The President could have stayed home and waited for the astronauts to reach the mainland. But if he had done that he would have missed a personal involvement. He capitalized, in a pseudo-event, on an immense drama that had captured the world's attention.

Perhaps the most sustained, and successful, application of the technique as a diversion from threatening attacks on a President's political flanks was represented by White House orchestration of the return of American prisoners of war from North Vietnam as a highly emotional extravaganza that the media, and the President's opponents, could neither ignore nor criticize.

Most of the full-time campaign consultants, who have become so numerous they recently formed their own professional association, have no doubt that these techniques can be employed to win state and national elections and to create new, major political figures virtually out of whole cloth. Tony Schwartz is a volatile and eccentric man, but after spending a morning viewing his wares and listening to his pitch, I found it hard to dismiss his claim: "With enough money, I can prepare commercials that will make anyone a household word in a single day." I would like to believe that there is still some distance between arrival at celebrity status and qualifying for high public office, but I have to concede that it is shrinking.

Schwartz has written a book extolling his powers, and has even displayed some of his prize creations before a congressional committee holding hearings on election reforms. However, there is not much evidence that this aspect of political advertising, as well as the obvious corruption of the enormous campaign funds required to pay for it, has yet attracted the serious attention it deserves.

Watergate, of course, has provided a spectacular demonstration of how influence inevitably follows campaign contributions right into the highest circles of government, corrupting everything, and everyone, it touches. It is to be hoped that key members of Congress also are beginning to understand the corollary lesson—that merely tightening existing devices intended to limit and publicize the source of campaign contributions cannot possibly halt practices so deeply embedded in our way of doing political business. The only way to end the money corruption is to remove the reason for it by providing for adequate public financing of political campaigns from the very beginning of the nominating process through the general election. The official machinery required to accomplish this also could eliminate the worst abuses of visceral political hucksterism, for the first principle of publicly financed campaigns ought to be that all candidates should be subject to equal exposure under common conditions. Properly handled, this would end the hired managers' ability to control the context of the presentation and reinstate the requirement that each candidate must literally speak for himself under conditions designed to serve the interests of an audience presumed to be seeking an opportunity to find out where he stands, as well as how he looks.

Externally, in the total development of mass communications, extraordinary technological possibilities also are emerging, and there is a great scramble for advantage in the potential markets that are presumed to be within sight with the advent of cable systems, video cassette playback machines, and even more innovative hardware already in being, if not yet in service. There are some who believe that the dominant role of the commercial networks inevitably will be recast in this process. While the potential is undoubtedly there for such a vast reshuffling of the power base, the remarkable capacity of the industry for delaying action so far leaves the odds with the extant communications conglomerates in any realistic appraisal of the new world a-comin'.

Harvey Wheeler, Senior Fellow at the Center, who regularly bends his skills as a political scientist to futurology, sketched in this broad-stroke outline of impending change in a paper for the Center conference:

A multi-media home is already technologically feasible—not the dwelling we already know, with radio, television, and tape recorders patched in, but an entirely new assortment of media installations with a revolutionary new domestic architecture to accompany it. Many of the electronic components are already available: systems for receiving, recording, storing, and reproducing all kinds of pictorial, printed, symbolic, and aural information. The rapidly developing cable facilities will make available enough channels so that almost anything desired can be tuned into a rationalized system. Pictorial, graphic, sound, and print media then can be considered as a whole, with all sources of knowledge theoretically accessible. Every existing data bank would be a reservoir to be drawn upon when needed.

Each person might then have the ability—or at least the possibility—of preprogramming his cultural environment for a period reaching far into the future. Adjustments in the programming mix could be made on a regular basis to comport with family and social changes, changing individual interests, and varying rates of development.

The political implications are evident. The multi-media home might provide the domestic foundation for the growth of a permanent counter-culture that could enable us to banish the most recalcitrant source of despotism, cultural deficiency. Multi-media programs employing operant conditioning techniques could be designed to lift the present cultural status of each person progressively so that the "subscriber" climbs the ladder of cultural excellence according to his capacity for assimilation. Of course, education and culture are only the minimum civic essentials; the home system also can embrace the entire range of human activities, providing for leisure, amusement, and frivolity according to individual desire.

All this is technologically possible today. The means are at hand to move toward the realization of one of man's oldest dreams: a society in which all citizens, the most lowly as well as the most favored, could enjoy the fruits of civilization.

The constitutional implications are profound. To bring this system into being we would have to confront the problems surrounding what Alexander Meiklejohn called a positive interpretation of the First Amendment: acceptance by the government of the obligation to facilitate the acculturation of citizens as well as to protect their freedoms. This, of course, is a realm fraught with danger, for it raises the specter of totalitarian thought control. Hence, a new and strengthened conception of the First Amendment would be necessary; one that protects not only the individual's "right to know," but his "right to be heard."

This is the acculturational potential of the future. It is made possible by the technological developments leading to the multimedia home; it is made necessary by the decivilizing and deculturizing forces now spreading unchecked throughout our mass-scale cities and bureaucracies; and it is made hazardous by the novel manipulative potentials it will embody.

These are the vastly changed conditions under which we now must consider the dictum of Alexander Hamilton, who in *The Federalist* wrote of the free press: ". . . its security, whatever fine declarations may be inserted in any constitution respecting it, must altogether depend upon public opinion, and on the general spirit of the people and of the government. And here, after all . . . must we seek the only solid basis for all our rights."

I would contend that the fine declaration embodied in the First Amendment by Hamilton's old adversary, Thomas Jefferson, has served us well, not only as a symbol but in the most practical way. There have always been strict constructionists on the Court who held, with the late Justice

Hugo Black, that when the Constitution said Congress shall pass *no* law inhibiting speech or press it meant exactly that. If jurists of this persuasion have never been in a majority, they have been influential enough to confine the Court's balancing tests within narrow limits. It is this essentially negative concept that has permitted, or perhaps required, what Harry Kalven termed the elegant gamble under which our national leaders have usually, if reluctantly, accepted freewheeling criticism, rhetorical disorder, and personal calumny as the price of democratic governance. The clear and present danger exposed in the wake of Watergate resulted from the fact that, in word and deed, Richard Nixon rejected that concept, and in doing so elicited, at least temporarily, the support of a majority of the people.

I have reached an age where I am most comfortable in the company of elders who nod sagely in the face of calamity and observe that we have been through all this before. And so we have, but not in the same way, nor on a comparable scale. It is pertinent to recall that a blue-jawed Wisconsin senator who styled himself Joe McCarthy buffaloed the free press and came close to imposing a deadly conformity upon a generation of Americans by recklessly charging treason against any who dissented from simplistic anti-Communism. But we also must recall that the Senator was a lone demagogue operating outside the real centers of power. The press, responding reflexively to his sensationalism, made possible his brief reign of terror. But when he exceeded the establishment's tolerance, the media—most notably through the probing eye of newborn television—also provided the means by which he was promptly cut down.

The latest attack on the national media has been orchestrated by a man sitting at the very center of executive power, and virtually certain to appoint a majority of his own choosing to the Supreme Court. Until Watergate pulled him up short, Richard Nixon moved openly to undercut the coequal status of the Congress. In this incarnation he has not professed to act against the kind of diaphanous domestic Communist conspiracy that served him well in his early politicking. He may or may not share the view of those impassioned administration spokesmen who contend that liberal journalists have seized control of the national media from their conservative proprietors. That conspiratorial figment, in any case, is incidental to the fact that the President found himself in position to exploit an evident backlash of public opinion against a decade of radical rhetoric and confrontation politics. The polarization produced by the unrestrained polemics of the young, the racial minorities, and the assorted "liberation" movements predictably resulted in a political division that leaves a substantial majority not only committed against drastic change but deeply resentful of the minority's strident attack upon its morality—and of the media which have borne home the hard truths and false charges.

In this atmosphere resort to the First Amendment may only result in formal reduction of its presumed reach. This was the case when appeal was made to the Burger Court for a ruling affirming the claim of reporters to immunity against enforced court testimony of the sort accorded doctors, priests, and lawyers. The new majority on the high court said no, and the result has been a shower of subpoenas in criminal and civil cases that require violation of newsmen's pledges of confidentiality to their sources, and a number of reporters have gone to jail for refusing to comply. In desperation, the media have turned to state legislatures and the Congress, seeking relief through "shield" laws.

The *New York Times*, which leads the field with its

splendid record of investigative reporting, has consistently displayed steady nerve under attack, as in the landmark Pentagon Papers case. But its managing editor, A. M. Rosenthal, now says this kind of journalism can't be continued under the present circumstances: "I say flatly that without the guarantee of confidentiality, investigative reporting will disappear. The erosion of confidentiality will mean the end of the exposure of corruption as far as the press is concerned."

There is an understandable tendency to dismiss such warnings from the media as self-serving. For almost a century leading newspapers and magazines have been major commercial enterprises as well as quasi-public institutions, and this has been the situation of the broadcasters from their beginning. On the business side, with rare exceptions, their record has not been characterized by a notable absence of cupidity. The contrast between high-flown claims of First Amendment immunity as tribunes of the people and the grubby practices of the countinghouse has always endowed the media's public image with an aura of hypocrisy. Having long ago abandoned any systematic criticism of each other's performance, except for the largely theatrical critique of TV programming by newspapers, they generally unite in condemnation of any outside agency that dares subject them to the kind of criticism they apply to every other enterprise colored with the public interest.

So it is they found themselves with few defenders in the face of their current encirclement. The assault from the radical left is *pro forma,* and the scorn of the intellectuals is traditional. Now there is even mutiny within the ranks. Most of the major cities have periodical journalism reviews devoted to exposing the mal- and misfeasance of local newspapers and broadcasters, and these are usually staffed anonymously by volunteers regularly employed by the media they criticize. Within the newsrooms the generational controversy has produced demands for the right of advocacy on the part of reporters as well as editors, and it is not uncommon for editorial employees to buy advertising space to dissociate themselves from the political positions taken on a newspaper's editorial page. The feisty national journalism review, (*More*), organized a counter-convention opposite the annual meeting of the American Newspaper Publishers Association as a memorial to the late A. J. Liebling, the irreverent press critic of *The New Yorker,* and drew participation from many well-known stars of the "straight" press. The second Liebling counter-convention was scheduled opposite the Washington meeting of the American Society of Newspaper Editors, with ASNE somewhat sheepishly joining in the arrangements.

Still, the old reflexes prevail. It is truly remarkable under these circumstances to find the broadcasters and publishers in the same ungainly position they occupied twenty-five years ago, when I described them as huddled, rumps together, horns out, against a proposal for a non-governmental and legally toothless press council to undertake systematic oversight of the performance of the media, and appraise the validity of the assaults against them. Whether resistance to the new National News Council will moderate, as it has under similar circumstances in Great Britain, remains to be seen. But surely the proposal deserves the most serious consideration, for—extralegal though it is, and must be—it offers the possibility of dealing *de facto* with the corrosive issues arising in the gray areas of conflict among the interests of government, media, and public. These have always existed, and I believe must exist if we are to maintain a media-government relationship that can be adversary when necessary and collaborative when all parties join in mutual respect and common cause.

There have always been unwritten rules, accepted, if not acknowledged, by both sides. Reporters have rarely gone to jail in the past for refusal to testify in court, because there was almost always a lawyers' compromise that met the requirements of justice without forcing a showdown test of the reporter's need for confidentiality against the judge's necessity to compel public testimony. Ironically, this was the issue, with the critical roles now played by the chief executive versus a combination of legislative and judicial interests, upon which Richard Nixon took the stand that forced a constitutional confrontation in the wake of Watergate.

The press has tacitly accepted the government's right to some secrets, and in military matters and cases of purely personal scandal has voluntarily helped keep them, even while refusing to acknowledge that any public official's act lies beyond the people's right to know. Although the law presumably cannot compel them to do so, the best newspapers scrupulously observe the principles of the Fairness Doctrine, and open their columns to those who have been defamed, and those who hold opposing political views. Newsmen, fated to be hired hands by the nature of their calling, can never attain true professional independence, but they do have standards of professional integrity recognized among themselves, and most often respected by their employers. There are no absolutes in this shadowy area, and in its own way the Supreme Court has recognized that this is so in its rulings on First Amendment cases.

This will be the domain of the National News Council. It is intended to provide a place where any outraged private citizen can bring his complaints against the media in expectation of an impartial hearing and a public finding; it also will be a place where the media themselves can seek a comparable hearing in the face of the attacks from their critics, inside and outside of government. There can be no forced testimony, no punishment, no fines, no imprisonment —the Council's only recourse is to public exposure, and its appeal is to tradition and to the industry's collective self-respect. Its most important function might well turn out to be the one not yet much talked about—to establish and maintain a standard of ethics which could, by informal means, guarantee the individual journalist the professional independence and recourse he requires to fulfill his function in a system where ownership and responsibility are increasingly diffused.

This may seem a frail defense against the enormous pressures generated by the power centers of government on the one hand and the temptations of the marketplace on the other, but at least it breathes the spirit of civility Alexander Hamilton proclaimed as the only solid basis for all our rights. And, after all, an effective forum for those who insist that robust debate on public affairs justifies the protection of the First Amendment was all the Founding Fathers promised when they laid in place their great monument to individualism as an indispensable bulwark of democracy.